For our mothers, Mimi Stamps and Mary von Wahlde,
our inspiration and our guides of the past.
And to our daughter, Emma, our hope for the future.

And to all of our dear friends who kindly allowed us to
photograph their houses, and share their worlds.

Stamps & Stamps
Style & Sensibility

Stamps & Stamps
Style & Sensibility

by Diane Dorrans Saeks

Photography by Kate Stamps

RIZZOLI
NEW YORK

Foreword

I first met Kate and Odom Stamps in the early 1990s, when I was living in Los Angeles. We were neighbors in Park La Brea, a sprawling apartment complex, and like them, I had a garden apartment— in a block of two-story painted brick boxes—that was sensibly designed, with a view of a communal lawn. That's where the similarities ended, however.

My living room was a mix of contemporary, vintage, and antique furniture and a few artworks, within the standard Park La Brea envelope of off-white walls and bare parquet floors. Kate and Odom's apartment, on the other hand, was a dream. The open living-dining area was painted a color that Kate described as "faded apricot/Tuscan pink," and beautiful fabrics and rugs complemented the elegant antique furniture, including a chest-on-chest atop which were pieces of wonderful eighteenth-century cream-ware. While the apartment had tremendous style, it was also unpretentious and welcoming. And, unlike my patio, with its little table, café chairs, and a sprinkling of potted plants, theirs had a canopy of passion flowers, and plenty of roses—a perfect, sheltered spot for an alfresco dinner.

Kate and Odom, I discovered, were intimidatingly smart, well-read, and well-traveled, yet they were down-to-earth, with a wonderful sense of humor. After I left Los Angeles in 1994, they bought a small house in South Pasadena and set about renovating it and creating a large garden. I might have visited the house once, soon after they bought it, but I did not see it completed until 2017.

In May of that year, I was traveling to Los Angeles, and Kate invited me to stay. Having known Kate for so long, I was familiar with her gift for decorating and her talent for combining beautiful objects and materials in a way that looks low-key and lived-in; she is one of the few American decorators working today who genuinely understands the English sensibility. Even so, I was amazed by what I saw.

Small by today's standards, the house proves that bigger isn't always better. I walked into the cozy sitting room, with its high ceiling and pine-plank paneling—products of Odom's architectural artistry—its comfortable sofas and chairs, its beautiful objects and art, and its seductive, high wall of books, and was instantly smitten. Since then, I have spent a number of evenings in that room, chatting with Kate and Odom over cocktails, or in their compact, impossibly chic dining room, savoring one of Kate's delicious meals. I've stayed in the Cabana, a tiny guest house with lots of books, charming furniture, and a view into the garden. And my reaction is always the same: I never want to leave.

That is, in part, thanks to Kate's philosophy of decorating. "I hate perfect rooms," she says. "I've always liked human rooms, with combinations of textures and paintings, and very comfortable seating. Even grand things shouldn't stand out." But this house also owes its charm to Odom's skill: By simply reallocating the interior spaces, including turning a large sleeping porch into three rooms, the house is effectively larger than it was before. "What Odom does is so rational, and so understated," Kate notes admiringly. Returning the compliment, Odom says, "I give Kate a good set of drawings, and she knocks it out of the park."

Stamps & Stamps is best known for its renovations of older houses in and around Los Angeles, and Odom is adept at working with the historical-revival styles that characterize much of the area's residential architecture. One of his professors at Tulane, the architect Eugene Cizek, helped Odom "understand how to look at a building, and the times that brought it about." And that makes it easy, he says, to "channel what the original architect would have done."

But Odom's interests also include modern and contemporary architecture. When he and Kate first arrived in Los Angeles, Odom saw many houses from the postwar Modernist era, by architects like John Lautner or firms like Buff & Hensman, or Smith &

Williams, whose founder, Whitney Smith, designed buildings that Odom particularly admires for their mastery of the relationship between indoors and out.

So while Odom's current projects include the design of a brick-clad, mansard-roofed house in Baton Rouge, Louisiana, that evokes "a French Colonial mews," he is also at work on the renovation and expansion of a contemporary travertine-clad house in Los Angeles that he designed in 1997, and which was influenced by vernacular Greek terraced houses. And in 2019, Odom completed another contemporary house, a clean-lined, airy structure, with ample daylight and views of the landscape, in South Pasadena. Whether they are working individually or together, Kate and Odom use their talents to design houses and interiors that prioritize the pleasures of domestic life over trends or aspiration. When you walk into one of their houses, you know you're home.

—Pilar Viladas

Table of Contents

Introduction by Diane Dorrans Saeks

A HOUSE, A GARDEN, AND A DREAM

Three decades ago, interior designer Kate Stamps, hand-in-hand with her young daughter, Emma, walked up the driveway of a mysterious South Pasadena house hidden among towering California oak trees. Emma had spied a dusty For Sale sign hidden among weeds. Their optimistic exploration marked the beginning of the family's romance with a house and a burgeoning career.

Beneath two noble carob trees and in poetic disrepair was a green-painted shingled Craftsman house built at the turn of the twentieth century. Created with integrity and fine materials, the house was waiting for Kate and her classically trained architect husband, Odom Stamps, and their passionate expertise.

"The moment I saw this cottage, I knew how we could make it into a home with character, soul, and comfort," recounts Odom.

The Stamps & Stamps philosophy has always been to take on a project in its totality, to perfectly calibrate and coordinate all facets of a beautiful residence. Harmony of the architecture, the interiors, and the gardens is essential to their belief that all aspects of a property must be conceived and executed with a clear vision of an integrated whole. This has been their approach to clients' houses as well as their own.

"We strive for ambience with authenticity, always returning to the very basics of good design," adds Kate.

They founded Stamps & Stamps in South Pasadena in 1991 and continue to collaborate closely. Their interiors have a solid and inspiring quality, a blurring of eras, a certain enchantment. Proportion and detail, scale and suitability, grace and lack of pretension are words they live by. Integrity of materials, functional design, and appropriateness are their guiding forces.

They enliven the spirit of the place, bestow a sense of humanity and charm. At every turn there's a comfortable chair, a down-filled sofa, a place to read a book, an elegant mantel, beautiful light, an air of repose, a dash of reckless bohemian abandon.

Odom's encyclopedic knowledge of every style and period has provided the harmonious architectural framework of their work. His flawless design makes rooms look effortless and uncontrived.

And in Kate's interiors there are echoes of Nancy Lancaster and John Fowler, Scandinavian country houses, esoteric Ottoman and Moroccan textiles, the plastered ceilings at Knole, the colors of Robert Adam, and Vita Sackville-West's rooms in the Tower at Sissinghurst. There's the eccentricity of the Bloomsbury Group, the flourish and poetry of Madeleine Castaing, allusions to Jane Austen and Virginia Woolf.

Rooms by Stamps & Stamps are the essence of comfort. The architecture and materials are simple, unforced. Down cushions require fluffing, fragrant garden flowers fill vases, lamps are turned on, candles lit. The elements of decoration are cohesive, evoking a literary dream, a longed-for ideal.

"A cup of tea solo, or a glass of wine with a friend, a book, a fire, a quiet moment or with music and singing, this is the way I hope all rooms can be," shares Kate.

And their fortunate clients live surrounded by just such daily pleasures of quiet luxuries and dreamy panoramas in rooms that delight, all qualities central to the Stamps & Stamps philosophy. The fine and handcrafted and rare things that fill these rooms are a visual feast, delicious and treasured, enjoyed daily and for years to come.

The House

Hidden from view beyond the overarching trunks and branches of massive carob trees and a tangle of fragrant jasmine hedges, the 1904 cottage where Kate and Odom Stamps have lived for the past three decades is their ultra-private universe, a vivid expression of their aesthetic ideals and their unwavering love of the classical world.

This designer and architect are lifelong Anglophiles, and both are obsessed with creating emotionally resonant interiors and heeding the finest points of architecture and antiques. Besotted by design history, they have enriched their house and garden to express their literary leanings, presenting their lifetime collections, their academic studies, and their vast knowledge of arcane building and craft techniques.

Kate and Odom's collections enhance each room. In every corner stand noble bookcases and bookshelves brimming with books, joyfully announcing their vocabulary of historic sources, neoclassical inspirations, and literary allusions.

The couple's love of art and their decades of travel to study late eighteenth-century English country houses have resulted in a home that's a perfect portrait of their passions and interests. They live in a richly imagined cottage that is elegant and harmonious, a little bohemian, romantic, joyfully expressive, unpretentious, original, and full of delight. It's their world, their creation.

Kate and Odom's house was originally built in 1904 as the carriage house of a grand South Pasadena estate. With a nod to the Arts and Crafts movement and Greene and Greene, the architecture included rooms for a handyman and a groom above two large carriage bays, and not much else.

After the estate was sold in the forties, the carriage house became a one-bedroom cottage with later informal additions. Odom's first focus was to reorganize, placing the front door in a logical position, enclosing porches. He designed an internal stair to provide access to the lower level and outdoor dining. A porch became a dining room, and all other rooms were reconfigured in a new floor plan.

"My concept was to keep the Greene and Greene style, and to maintain a feeling of a cottage in a large garden," says Odom. "Very little structural change was involved, and the exterior style and appearance were carefully altered, and yet we nearly doubled the living area to 1,900 square feet."

New windows were added to reveal the trees that flourish right up to the house. Pittosporums, oaks, and citrus trees seem to be reaching into the windows. Kate and Odom spent the first decade nurturing the garden while slowly making architectural improvements.

The sitting room had always been part of the 1904 structure, and Odom discovered useable attic space above the ceiling. He raised the ceiling to take advantage of the height there and added a fireplace, which is the gracious focal point. He had the sitting room walls covered with painted and umber-glazed pine planking installed vertically, in a nod to the original utilitarian structure. "The sitting room is big enough to feel open and generous, but small enough to feel intimate," says Kate.

After three decades, every room in this house, except the dining room, is full of books. The ambience is a literary mystery. Is this Southern California or a remote corner of Kent or Norfolk or Shropshire?

A brick path winds through the garden. It was crafted using broken bricks repurposed by Odom from building sites. It's elegant, and the bricks were free. Visits to their magical cottage require attentive choreography among arching hydrangeas, a tangle of climbing roses, glistening cobwebs, swooping branches, and jungly leaves and fuchsias that swing into view.

Hidden sculptures, secret groves, and exuberant splashes of color add to the many pleasures of finding the front entrance. Kate's dense and creative planting for more than three decades includes fuchsia, white dogwood, citrusy Philadelphus coronarius with delicate white flowers, brunnera with colorful heart-shaped leaves, and bursts of white/pink oak leaf hydrangea, a favorite. Kate's plants flourish in the cooling shelter of tall sycamores and native oaks high overhead. At ground level, with a good watering system, and care by an excellent gardener, this harmonious landscape fares very well even in South Pasadena's baking summers with temperatures often soaring well above 100 degrees Fahrenheit. Winters are fresh but rarely frosty. Her trees and flowers are very healthy and robust and all artfully placed, with ferns under-planted and moist, and hydrangeas perfectly shaded.

Surrounded by ferns, camellia, and abutilon, the entrance hall and a corner of the sitting room come into view as guests approach the front door. The entrance hall is full of light filtered through the surrounding garden. A graceful mahogany saber-legged chair is Scottish, and upholstered in green tufted leather.

On summer evenings, Kate and Odom throw open the windows to welcome gentle breezes, and the scent of moist leaves and spicy bark and Philadelphus wafts through the room.

Kate loves to pick flowers from her garden, including plumbago, the cupped "Alnwick" rose by English rose breeder David Austin, Corydalis, and Campanula. Their intense fragrance drifts into the air, a delicious welcome and mood enhancer for guests.

The English chest-on-chest secretary of plum pudding mahogany was a gift from Odom's mother, an antique dealer. Slipcovered in one of Christopher Moore's toiles, the armchair is a favorite spot for morning coffee. The oval-backed painted chair, in the style of Scottish architect Robert Adam. is from the late eighteenth century, Kate's favorite period. Kate mixed the wall paint in a custom green-ocher-umber and lampblack mix and applied it with a dry brush for a soft plaster finish.

Previous pages: Kate designed the sitting room to be the essence of comfort. Facing east and south, the sitting room feels as if it is perched among the oaks and carobs and a fifty-year-old Viburnum suspensum. Kate values ambience, blurring eras and creating a dreamscape of muted colors and shadowy silhouettes. Immutable daily actions are performed here. Fresh flowers adorn tables. Down cushions require fluffing, each lamp must be turned on or off in its turn. All of the elements of decoration are strong, but none dominates. On each side of the windows hang hand-colored Francesco Bartolozzi engravings of Hans Holbein and his wife, circa 1795. The original Holbein oil portraits, painted in 1540, are in the Queen's Gallery, part of the Royal Collection.

The fireplace is Irish, eighteenth-century, in carved box-wood with classical motifs. "It is unpretentious, perfect for a cottage, and we loved the fine carving," says Kate. Above the mantel is a large-scale Italian watercolor of Cremona cathedral. On the mantel are Annabelle hydrangeas,

feverfew, and plumbago in eighteenth-century Bristol painted glass vases. In the corner, the bar is orchestrated on an English mahogany chest, circa 1780, surrounded by a collection of gilt-framed Spanish paintings. The lamp is a Persian painted metal vase.

Above & opposite: A Surrealist Hermés paperweight/ magnifying glass from Marché Paul Bert at the Saint-Ouen flea market in Paris is on a table by Jamb topped by specimen marble.

The pinecones were a lucky find on a winter snow trip with their daughter, Emma, in the San Jacinto Mountains.

Kate has created harmony among the disparate materials, colors, and textures in the sitting room. The eight-foot-wide sofa is slipcovered in Rose Tarlow herringbone weave in a soft nutmeg hue. The curtains are panels of Indonesian Sumba cotton ikat. The sofa pillows are a mix of eighteenth-century French woven silk and antique ikat.

Above: A large English mahogany breakfast table with drawers holds silver-framed family photographs.

Opposite: The down-filled six-foot-long sofa by Stamps & Stamps is covered in a silk chenille velvet. A collection of gilt-framed watercolors shows English, Egyptian, and European scenes, hung high to emphasize the soaring twelve-foot ceiling. Kate notes that the sitting room is a space that she can enjoy alone, or with a cocktail gathering, or just the family beside the fire. "We have the pleasure of welcoming family and friends," she says. "A cup of tea, a flute of Champagne, one of Odom's famous Sazerac cocktails, or a glass of rare wine, an old book, a fire, a quiet moment, or an evening of music or singing. Private or celebratory. Versatile. Welcoming. This is the way I hope all rooms can be."

Opposite: Kate believes in the English design concept of creating "a whack of black" to give a room a dramatic dimension and graphic silhouette. The Chinese ebonized dragon bench, elaborately carved, brings the richness of a distant culture to this bookish world.

Above: The end table has an antique Italian metallic silk cover. The pottery pitcher is by Martin Homer, Ludlow, Shropshire, a favorite of Kate's.

Following pages: The sitting room has become a library, full of books on antiques, art, decoration, textiles, and architecture. Books from Chinoiserie to Baroque to Axel Vervoordt and Potsdam, and from the Bosphorus and Brunelleschi to Hepplewhite and Renzo Mongiardino are arranged by topic. Books are numbered by shelf so that they are easy to find and replace.

Previous pages: A Japanese lacquer cabinet, circa 1740, was crafted for the English market; its stand was made later in the Chinese Chippendale style. Its sixteen drawers contain Kate's collections of historic black-and-white photography. On top sits a pair of English opaline glass cornucopia vases along with English decalcomania glass balls. The painting is a "sacred and profane" tribute to Bacchus, a New Orleans Mardi Gras tradition.

Above & opposite: In the dining room, casement windows (with almost invisible screens) are flung open all summer. Walls are horizontal pine planks, glazed in a persimmon tone with seven layers of glaze applied. Pelmets of French toile with a guilloche trim disguise the low ceiling height and dress up the window without the fussiness of curtains.

The dining room measures just 9 feet by 12 feet but feels larger, thanks to the large-scale chairs and the generously proportioned round table. On the table is a virtuoso combination of mismatching block-printed cotton. Kate's collection includes eighteenth-century blue-green Bristol glasses and an English 1815 pitcher with scenes of Istanbul, which she uses as a water jug. Garden flowers are arranged in an eighteenth-century German painted glass tankard.

Kate and Odom are classicists to the core, and their stairway gallery of architectural drawings, grisaille renderings, watercolors, and measured sketches are their tribute to influential neoclassical British architect Sir John Soane (1753-1837). Andrea Palladio is also honored with a drawing of a sixteenth-century villa in the Veneto he designed. Also featured are a sepia painting of the Colosseum in Rome, a sketch of the exterior of Chartres cathedral, and a floor plan of Ely cathedral. Kate favors spare black or gilt frames, keeping the effect very simple and austere. Among architectural fragments on display are stone columns, alabaster models of the Duomo and the Leaning Tower of Pisa, and a cork model of the Tower of London in a glass box.

Above: Softly filtered light in Kate's studio creates a calm mood for an afternoon of watercoloring. An avid painter since school days, Kate first sketches with fine lead pencils, then adds a wash of watercolor to render exquisitely detailed images of trees and leaves. Renderings of clients' interiors, drawn to scale, are often on her painting table.

Opposite and following pages: Center stage is a charming cream and teal 1760 tea-height rococo German table with an intricate glass beadwork top in grisaille tones. An early nineteenth-century suzani is from Christie's auction house in London. The pair of cane-backed French chairs and the French daybed were a Louisiana find. The quirky pair of Italian sconces on concave bases are trimmed with jade flowers, all slightly wonky and charming.

Above: Odom designed the reeded bookcases to give a sense of architecture and definition to the tiny room. "Book collections add so much to our rooms," says Kate. "The only room in our house without books is the dining room." With a cup of jasmine tea and a book she's passionate about, Kate may spend a quiet afternoon here, dreaming of new designs.

Opposite: The writing desk has secret compartments for pens, writing paper, cards, and billets-doux. The silhouette of Emma Stamps, aged eight, in the eighteenth-century style is by an unknown talented artist.

In Kate's bedroom, the eighteenth-century *lit à la polon-aise* includes vertical posts that support metal arms swooping upward to support the wooden cornice. South Pasadena is earthquake country, so Kate suspended the cornice from the ceiling with sturdy wires in each corner. Swags of Tissus d'Hélène' "Eloise," a rose-printed cotton, have a soft tea-dyed effect. "I found this romantic print in London and immediately had to have it," says Kate, who used fifty yards to upholster the head- and footboard as well. The curtains are lined with cream matte silk. "You have to be decisive and bold with a lit à la polonaise," says Kate. "You have to be generous with the fabric to get the full effect of this dramatic bed style." The bedcover is embroidered cotton by Chelsea Textiles. The Colefax and Fowler bedside table, painted by George Oakes, is ornamented with trompe-l'oeil leaves and branches.

Above and opposite: Kate's dressing table is decorated with silk taffeta with ruched antique velvet trim, found in London at Hilary Batstone Antiques near Pimlco Road. Kate dressed the table with favorite pieces including painted glass, perfume boxes, crystal, photos, eighteenth-century Bilston enameled candlesticks, and a delicate French straw-work box. The mirror is Venetian, found at auction in New Orleans.

Following pages: The tall window overlooks a quiet corner of the garden, filled with lavender and Iceberg roses.

Window curtains are Prelle handwoven silk, lined with a light matte silk. They are finished with "Délicat" silk fan-edged gimp, a classical trim by Samuel & Sons, a favorite trim specialist Kate works with often. Walls are glazed in pale blue, slightly grayed down with a soft glaze.

The gold-framed pastel portrait, French, eighteenth century, hangs above a French needlework sampler and a bedside table from designer Nancy Lancaster's apartment, which was located above what once were the Colefax and Fowler offices on Avery Row in London.

Kate designed Odom's bedroom suite as an ultra-comfortable retreat and haven after a long day of travel. With its lovely view out into the garden, it is a library, a study, a bedroom, a TV room, and a respite from summer heat.

The substantial curtained bed cabinet was inspired by sixteenth-century English and European country house bedroom cabinets enclosed to keep out drafts. Odom's is framed with antique French fruitwood in a design of baskets and flowers. The dramatic antique Spanish parcel-gilt bedstep, possibly originally from a room in a chapel of a religious order, is now used as an impromptu bookcase.

The floor is covered with a patchwork of carpets, each with a different provenance and pattern, all vivid and compelling. They are placed on top of seagrass matting. The table is eighteenth-century Dutch, tile topped and with black-painted legs. The bed curtains are a substantial French nineteenth-century wool and silk stripe. Bennison "Bird and Basket" printed linen was chosen for the slipcovered chair and ottoman, each finished with a box-pleated skirt.

Opposite: In the twilight, russet curtains of nineteenth-century English silk and wool mohair frame casement windows with views of fig and avocado trees. The walls are covered in bookshelves with volumes on history, philosophy, and architecture. The tapestry-covered chair is French, nineteenth century.

Above: The seventeenth-century Flemish tapestry hangs on an iron rod, screening shelves of paperback books. The carved wood lotus lamp from Goa turns to make the petals open. It was discovered by Kate at Piers Woodnutt in London.

S&S Garden

Kate and Odom Stamps's two-acre estate is private and a little mysterious. From the outside, there's no sign of their glorious rose bowers, parterres, welcoming house, Bell Cottage, or Cabana. Dramatic California native oaks soar overhead, suggesting an historic domain. The quiet avenue of elegant camphor and liquidambar street trees in South Pasadena gives little hint of what hides behind their simple wooden gates. But then the intense, exotic fragrance of brugmansia and heirloom roses and lavender wafts on the warm air and calls a visitor onward.

Handsome and iconic river rock (we call it arroyo stone) walls and vivid arching fireworks of pyracantha surround their Craftsman-style green wooden garden gate, and beyond it is the first intriguing sighting of Kate and Odom's glorious and unexpected landscape. Stepping through the green painted gate is like wandering into another country, an earlier era. Tall sycamores and cedars reach into the sunshine. Loquat-shaded borders and densely planted jasmine hedges offer privacy, and the house and two cottages are not revealed at first.

Paths of brick and gravel plunge through ferns, and then along a brilliant tapestry of pink and white roses, Oriental lilies, and overgrown brugmansia in golden bloom. Cream-flowered Osmanthus fragrans and Kate's delphiniums and foxgloves tower and arch on either side. There are literary and traditional English influences. Kate has spent many springs and summers exploring the great gardens of England, and her love for the gardens of Gertrude Jekyll and Vita Sackville-West is evident in her skillful and artful planting.

Like Sackville-West at Sissinghurst, Kate likes plants to fill every inch of the garden, with roses growing up and over arches, clematis twisting into the branches of trees, and ivy climbing up oaks and sycamores. Sage and marjoram scramble along paths, artichokes arch over terraces, plumbago tumbles over fences and arbors. Iceberg roses flourish here.

Odom and Kate planned a dramatic scene with a hundred-foot-long double border, filled with plectranthus, campanula, euphorbia, viburnum and macaya, magenta Geranium maderense, and loropetalum in joyful profusion. It's a sensual tangle of beauty and fragrance. Perennials do very well in this beautifully maintained garden, alongside a selection of annuals. There are abutilon, star jasmine, pink and cerise camellia, osmanthus, and white Nicotiana sylvestris, Sackville-West favorites. Bees feast. Hummingbirds hover.

Kate has studied the Southern California gardens of Florence Yoch and Lucile Council, all very architectural and elegant, and she admires American landscape designer Beatrix Farrand, the niece of Edith Wharton. Farrand, a noted colorist and bold plantswoman who pioneered the use of native plants, designed some of the notable gardens in Southern California.

Kate and Odom started planning the garden as soon as they acquired the property. Deep trenches were excavated, soil was amended, and drainage and an efficient watering system were planned to protect the trees and plants through the long dry summer.

Beyond the house there's a sheltered vegetable and herb garden where Kate can pick mint for Odom's cocktails. There are fresh tomatoes for a salad lunch, and later overripe figs to set on a platter of cheeses. Hidden beyond Bell Cottage is a citrus orchard, with crops of lemons, grapefruit, and oranges that flourish year-round.

The gardens honor several denizens of the South, including the delightful hydrangea quercifolia (oakleaf hydrangea), which has grown into a tall hedge near the Bell Cottage and has spread over the meandering path near the house. Its flowers, white with a blush of pink, seem to bloom almost year-round.

Heirloom climbing roses in palest pink and peach, and a century-old purple wisteria, add vertical interest. They love the protection from the trees. Kate likes the garden to look lush, and the planting to feel extravagant, with borders overbrimming with delicious scented leaves such as mint, rosemary, and rose-and nutmeg-scented geranium. Foliage is admired and selected and planted with as much care as every flower.

With the sunlit tops of oak branches far overhead, it is cool and fresh below. It's quiet save for the rustling of leaves, the sighing of sycamores, and perhaps a camellia leaf falling.

The estate is surrounded by historic arroyos (boulder-strewn dried river beds), and wildlife roam, slipping through hedges and gates, in search of prey. Sometimes at night, the howl of a roaming coyote or two adds a frisson to the peaceful scene. Little birds chirp and fret, and sometimes on hot summer days, seedpods crackle and brittle twigs whirl in the air.

Wildlife love this natural world. And for Kate and Odom, the estate is their ultimate escape, a personal expression, and a reward for expert plant selections and nurturing over three decades. Inspiration and beauty, indeed.

Bell Cottage

Hidden within the cool deodar cedar-shaded depths of the Stamps and Stamps estate, Bell Cottage is the rapturous embodiment of an English architectural folly. A petite guesthouse with a quirky flourish of Carpenter Gothic to the entry porch, it comprises an octagonal study / dining room, and a sitting room / bedroom with a soaring twelve-foot ceiling overlooking the family's citrus orchard. It acquired its name when Kate and Odom's daughter, Emma, moved into the guesthouse with her new husband, Andrew Bell.

Every inch of its 760 square feet has been deftly planned by Odom and Kate as a hideout with a thoughtful sense of luxury. It's decorative and is luxuriously appointed with a mini-refrigerator, secret closets, a sunny bathroom, a neat kitchen, kettles and teapots, coffee makers, and a tray of liquors all close at hand.

French doors open to a sheltered raised porch enclosed by a Carpenter Gothic pierced wood railing with interlocking circles and quatrefoils and with pike-topped newel posts. It's a romantic retreat and a welcoming residence.

"Bell Cottage is one of my favorite sets of rooms I have ever decorated," says Kate. "Odom and I originally designed it for ourselves and built it from the ground up, so it is a complete concept with a highly detailed interior, a vision of our personal engagement. We executed mostly as we wished."

A lovely folly, arboreal and camouflaged within the century-old garden, was their concept. On wild adventures across the English countryside, Odom and Kate have long admired whimsical architectural fantasies built in remote and bosky corners of grand estates. They wanted this same out-of-time feeling of escape for their guesthouse.

Odom sited the cottage among a tangle of fragrant white stephanotis, pink camellias, white "Annabelle" hydrangeas, graceful Viburnum plicatum, and a grand queen palm. The exterior is board and batten painted pale slate/green, and the roof is shingled. It's silent beneath noble sycamore trees and native oaks.

Inspired by the eighteenth-century English Gothic Revival movement and Carpenter Gothic styles in America in the nineteenth century, Odom planned the rooms and architecture for surprise and delight. The octagonal room to the west has Gothic-inspired double casement windows with trefoil arched spandrel panels above. Gothic-arched operable shutters modulate the light. The interior stair hall has a bold gothic arch formed-plaster opening modeled from measured drawings of an aisle window surround from the Gothic church in Sleaford, Lincolnshire, England.

The efficient kitchen has a true Gothic arched window and a refrigerator concealed in the Gothic cabinet. The bathroom has a steam shower and water closet chamber separated from the bathtub and sink cabinet and the most elaborate repeated Gothic paneling, particularly noticeable on the tub base and similar to the exterior detailing, the design enhanced by the repetition.

The drawing room / bedroom has a daybed that doubles as a deep sofa, as well as comfortable upholstered furniture. Odom and Kate are thoughtful hosts who have hidden secret clothes storage in the decorative paneling, designed multipurpose furniture, and created a deep sense of privacy.

At night, surrounded by fragrant stephanotis and jasmine, and in the deep embrace of the garden, Bell Cottage is just a flicker of candlelight, very mysterious. A festive dinner in the Octagon room is a magical experience.

Annabelle hydrangea blooms flourish along the path leading to the cottage. Guests arrive at Bell Cottage beneath the leafy porch and into the dramatic high-ceilinged Octagon, full of light and Gothic style. Odom and Kate planned it to work as a dining room, a library, a study, a place for reading and reverie, and even an extra sleeping room. Odom devised the Gothic arch doors and the ten-foot-tall bookcases as an architectural ensemble. The bookcase doors are lined in French chicken wire.

Plaster molding around the door is hand formed. The English oak table, circa 1840, was designed by Augustus Pugin, the pioneer of nineteenth-century Gothic Revival. Six chairs of burled fruitwood are German, circa 1830. The ikat silk on the pillows is from the Grand Bazaar in Istanbul. Silken seagrass on the floor adds to the timeless mood. The French chandelier has vivid turquoise opaline glass, positioned in a tin frame with crystal prisms.

"I've always loved the Gothic style," says Kate. "I grew up in the Midwest, where there are so many wonderful Carpenter Gothic houses, and I spent my young childhood in one of those. Later I lived in England, where the Gothic taste and architecture have been an influence on revival styles since the eighteenth century. I wanted to transplant a little of it to Southern California."

During the day, the pale cream Joa's White emulsion wall paint by Farrow & Ball has a soft pale taupe effect with a slight apricot cast.

"I selected this wall color because it is subtle and mutates with the reflection of leaves to an almost pale gold in the sunset," says Kate. Kate designed each angle of the Octagon room to serve several purposes and to offer a harmonious and logical roomscape. One angle of the Octagon is set up for study or writing, with a painted English Regency desk from English dealer James Graham-Stewart. The English Gothic bobbin chair is from 1820. The painted chair, with an original painted rush seat, was in the collection of Stanley Falconer, a Colefax and Fowler decorator who inherited it from John Fowler.

Above and opposite: A painted ocher and teal English pine chest of drawers from James Graham-Stewart is used to store bar glasses, crystal, tableware, and silver. The handcrafted, patinated tin tray is arranged as a practical bar. For a cocktail party, Kate and Odom bring in a large antique silver ice bucket, silver baskets of limes and lemons, and sprigs of mint from the garden.

Following pages: Kate designed a pair of ultra-deep armless sofas, which can quickly be arranged with bed linens for extra guests. They are covered in George Spencer strié velvet in teal blue. The elongated center pillows of eighteenth-century Turkish çatma cut silk velvet with metal-thread embroidery are crafted in Anatolia. The Turkish printed cotton textile wall hanging has ikat backing and binding.

Previous pages: A French neoclassical daybed is dressed in an Italian scalloped silk damask coverlet and an Azerbaijani suzani. As this is a living room by day and sleeping room by night, the bed is also a luxurious deep sofa. The floral painting is a family heirloom, hung between a pair of framed French eighteenth-century embroidered waistcoat panels. The nailhead-trimmed screen offers privacy and controls light. The chair, on casters, is covered with floral chintz with a skirt at "ankle

length" to reveal the delicate painted legs. The antique Moroccan rug adds another dimension to the decoration.

Above and opposite: Simple and elegant curtains are cutwork and hand-embroidered cotton and linen. The sofa is upholstered in custom "Fez Weave" by Guy Goodfellow. A pair of Napoleon III stools are covered in red and black Moroccan leather.

Opposite: On the French wine-tasting table, from Tom Stansbury Antiques, which has a marble top, afternoon tea is set with a fern motif English tea service. The eighteenth-century Dutch sidechair is covered with cerise Italian silk damask. The faux bamboo chair was acquired from the estate of John Fowler.

The eighteenth-century English oak fall-front secretary is an heirloom from Kate's mother's collection. The living room ceiling is twelve feet tall, so Kate arranged a pair of urns on capitals, along with framed vintage ikats, and English chargers on rococo walnut brackets to enhance the verticality.

Above: For the exterior of the cottage, Odom added Gothic details and a terrace. Hydrangeas flourish here beneath deodar cedar trees.

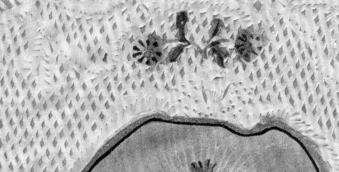

S Barbara

The Cabana

The Cabana, perfectly sited beneath two handsome century-old carob trees and surrounded by a filigree of lavender and Iceberg roses, is an ultra-private guest cottage within the verdant tangle of Kate and Odom's garden. The cozy interior embodies Virginia Woolf's ideal of "a room of one's own." It's an excellent haven for writers, readers, sleepers, and dreamers. And this one has Wi-Fi, a TV, and every possible tech amenity, along with a refrigerator and teakettle, all concealed of course.

Measuring a petite 270 square feet, the Cabana is lavished with all the comfort, style, and attention Kate and Odom give to the mansions on their client roster. There's seagrass matting covered with Oriental carpets, and notable landscape paintings, books, and a crewelwork-covered wing chair for reading. Even the flowers, freshly picked and fragrant, are reminiscent of the lavish garden bouquets Vita Sackville-West placed on her study desk in the tower at Sissinghurst.

Built in 1904 and the oldest structure on the Stamps' property, the Cabana was originally a garden shed and later a studio. The two massive, sheltering carobs have grown around it, their shade both cooling and soothing the guests within.

Odom has deployed all of his artistry and architectural sleight of hand to give the petite cabin a sense of spacious wonder and repose. After a deft redesign of the original footprint, Odom raised the ceiling to reveal the roof beams and bestow the interior with a strong architectural feeling. He kept the silhouette of the old structure, true and authentic to its origins.

Large French doors in the sitting room draw all-day light into the Cabana. They are centered on the brick steps that lead to a shady lavender-edged copse of fig trees, native oaks, and tall white flowering ligustrum. "French doors with large glass panes like ours hail from grand chateaux and Parisian palaces yet can be perfectly at home in a humble American cottage," notes Odom. Framed by voluminous cream linen hand-embroidered Chelsea Textile curtains that modulate summer sunlight, the outward-opening doors offer a gracious entrance and give the sitting room/bedroom an expansive feeling. Bookcases fill the walls on either side and above the door, framing it with an outline of cornices that form the outline of the peaked ceiling.

There are board games, chess, a handpicked library of art books and literature, and a spacious desk where Kate always places rose bouquets. "We maximized the bedroom/sitting room space, and created a lovely bathroom and dressing room for friends who might stay a little longer," says Kate. The pretty bathroom has a shower and claw-foot bath, originally in Odom's family home in New Orleans.

And when research and writing a chapter of the next great novel are completed, the bed is a dream, with an old-fashioned handmade cotton mattress and a cloudlike topper, heirloom monogrammed linen sheets, and a handcrafted quilt. The wooden bed frame is walnut, colonial, and carved in scrolls on the headboard and footboard. It's not unusual for guests to sleep until noon.

"There are things I love in that room that came from my childhood house in Michigan," says Kate. "The small-scale wing chair, upholstered in the same off-white crewel since the 1970s, sat in front of one of the arched Italianate windows in the upstairs hall of our house."

White and blue hydrangeas and Iceberg roses are in bloom for much of the year, and they provide a pretty frill around the almost-hidden shingled Cabana. It's private and quiet here. A brick path meanders from the main house and through the garden, a distance that provides a certain writerly solitude for guests. Except on cooler days of December and January, guests enjoy morning tea and coffee outdoors in the garden throughout the seasons.

Above and opposite: Everything is comfortable and in its place. The large, shallow nineteenth-century English cabinet, bought from James Graham-Stewart in London, that sits in the center of the long wall was constructed around a Georgian mahogany door, now painted a chalky cream. In this tiny space, the "Narnia Cabinet" poses the question, What will you find when you open the door? A passage through to C.S. Lewis's fantasy world? Instead, guests find collections of antique linens. Bold carpets, figurative oil paintings, and the quilt on the bed provide a colorful counterpoint to the cream-colored walls and curtains and keep the room in balance.

Following pages: Confident in the maxim that large furniture in a small room makes the interior feel more spacious, Kate added a luxurious and immensely comfortable bed and dressed it boldly with a colorful (and warm) array of quilts, blankets, antique embroidered sheets, and large pillows.

Kate's mother's small eighteenth-century English oak lowboy is now a versatile desk/dining table opposite the bed. It works well for afternoon tea and old-fashioned letter writing. The Italian eighteenth-century portrait of a mother and her children that adorned the sitting room in Kate's childhood home in Michigan hovers above the desk.

Santa Monica
Mediterranean

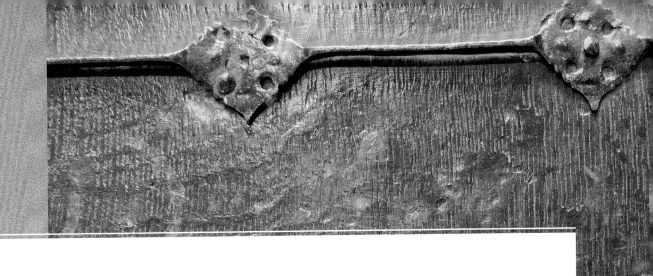

Longtime clients of Stamps & Stamps acquired a spacious and sunny house in Santa Monica, one of the loveliest parts of greater Los Angeles. It's near the sea and has ocean breezes that keep year-round temperatures fresh and cooler than inland parts of the city. "Location, in Los Angeles, is everything, and this one was beautiful," says Kate. "Architecture can be modified, interiors can be re-designed. But location is paramount, so we took the vaguely Spanish colonial spec house built in the early '90s and gave it coherent character, subtly pushing it toward a more substantial Tuscan style."

The owners weren't planning to do much real structural change, so they focused on the elements that would transform the house and make it feel authentic after crossing through the garden gate. For speed and efficiency, most of the alterations were internal. Odom's approach with the architecture was to focus on repurposing spaces, moving windows for better light and interior balance, aligning doorways. "I used restraint and balance to make quiet changes, and improve flow, and bring logic to room place-ment," he says. "In the end, shaping the interiors to make them cohesive and focused made a profound difference."

To give the interiors more character, Odom added moldings and trim, and Kate found several beautiful-ly detailed Italian marble and stone chimney pieces made in the early eighteenth century.

The biggest architectural changes were in the bedrooms on the second floor. Kate had wood floors installed to replace wall-to-wall Berber carpet. They added cornices and moldings throughout.

Kate and Odom combined two tiny bedrooms into a suite of rooms. The feminine new bedroom and sitting room are now joined by a pair of wide pocket doors. When there are no guests, the room doubles in size and has light from two sides. The shiny alder floors were painted with a pattern that echoes the reclaimed eighteenth-century Italian tile in the bathroom for some continuity in the space. "The owners are devoted readers and book collectors, so we installed bookcases everywhere, including built-in ones down all of the halls, in the offices, and on the landing, and even up the staircase," says Kate.

Kate and Odom surrounded the house with an Italian-style garden including an olive grove, ligustrum and box hedges, and a central quatrefoil fountain visible from the living room.

With a series of architectural changes completed, the decorating started. Kate first focused on floor coverings. All of the rugs in this house are exception-al, and they all came from Kate's favorite carpet dealer, Y & B Bolour, in the design district of Los Angeles. The sitting room has a magnificent late seventeenth-century Isfahan Polonaise carpet. It is beautifully worn in most places; just a little of the silk and metallic thread remain to show the glorious original color. The other is a fragment of a Persian carpet that complements the larger one perfectly.

"I love to use multiple carpets in a room, as they add character and color and bold pattern," says Kate. "Very old carpets have a special quality, one of gentle mellowness along with a kind of strength and grandeur. They don't work in every room because they cannot take tremendous wear, but when they find a good home they are always the most elegant element in a room."

High on the walls, the urns are Cypriot, from the fourth century BCE. They are securely attached to brackets backed by subtle wall hangings of the English Arts and Crafts period, woven by hand of Philippine abaca, silk, and linen. The room is comfortable and friendly, perfect for an evening with friends and family, or an afternoon with a good book.

The dramatic sitting room welcomes guests with soft upholstery, clerestory windows, warm integral-color plaster walls, and beautiful textiles. The fabrics are strong and quiet, designed to be background elements so that the carpets and objects shine. They also provide a soft counterpoint to the hand-printed damask pattern on wool and hemp created by fabric designer Sabina Fay Braxton for the Howard sofa. Placed in front of the arched window, the sofa is splendid, a modern take on eighteenth-century textiles. On closer inspection, other details come into focus, like the fifteenth-century Venetian petite carved lionesses, the bookcases with hand-tooled leather trim, the painted Regency chair (a model after Thomas Hope), and the exquisite circa 1720 Persian needlework on the cushions.

One of the biggest changes to the interiors was to remove the fireplace surrounds, which were craftsman with Batchelder-style tiles that were at odds with the nominally Mediterranean style of the house. Kate found elegant and boldly delineated neo-classical marble and stone chimney-pieces, Italian, from the early eighteenth century.

The new mantels and the elegant proportions of the fireplace surround give the room a composed feeling and set the tone for collections and Persian carpets. As the windows are a curious amalgam of styles and sizes, Kate decided against curtains and simply covered the glass with ultraviolet-blocking film to protect the furniture and objects. The concept is for the house to be full of strong, architectural pieces, with views of beautiful pine and bay trees giving a sense of privacy and tranquility.

Previous pages: The sitting room opens onto a small, circular entrance hall and to a courtyard terrace.

In the hall, a pair of seventeenth-century Portuguese side chairs from Balzac Antiques await the mail or a briefcase, too fragile for human occupants.

Above and opposite: Dining rooms are rarely used these days, but as this one is so prominently placed in the house and needs to fulfill its purpose occasionally, it's important that it looks good and functions efficiently. The table, from Ann Koerner in New Orleans, has extension leaves that pull out, and the chairs are new, made by Howe in London. They are strong and substantial to with-

stand the twenty-first-century guest in a way that pretty eighteenth-century chairs may not. They are covered in a blue silk damask and trimmed with hand-made gimp from Watts and Co. in London, a company that has been making fine silks and trimmings since 1874.

The large chest that holds neatly folded linens is Italian walnut, Tuscan, from about 1700. The hand-embroidered curtains from Chelsea Textiles have a refined, elegant beauty and are the perfect counterpoint to the jewel-toned eighteenth-century Turkish Oushak carpet. All the strong colors and shapes and distinctive dark furniture are in subtle balance, with no one element dominating.

Previous pages: Using muted but rich colors, Kate has turned a small bedroom into a Venetian fever dream. The bedspread is Persian, and the pillows are made with Sumba ikats from Indonesia. Velvet wall panels custom-printed by textile designer Sabina Fay Braxton frame Fortuny green-and-gold curtains, adding to the sensual mood. The hanging lanterns are Venetian. The deeply carved ornament with elaborate brackets that hangs above the bed is Venetian, parcel gilt, perhaps from a private chapel, circa 1740. Lined with silk brocade and silver gilt fringe, it's a whimsical element. The pair of folding inlaid Syrian tables were made to be easily transported with bases that are hinged and tops that pop off so they can be packed flat.

Opposite: The small étagère is English, Arts and Crafts, circa 1890, from James Graham-Stewart in London.

Above and opposite: The sitting room is papered with a fabulous Mauny wallpaper, designed by Marie Laurencin in 1912. The French nineteenth-century chair is covered in a burgundy silk velvet from Sabina Fay Braxton and embellished with hand-embroidered panels of silk floss from Namay Samay. The floors are painted to echo the Italian eighteenth-century floor tiles in the suite's bathroom.

Following pages: The curtains in the bathroom are in fabric by Robert Kime and Namay Samay. The delicate Italian eighteenth-century beadwork sconces are from Balzac Antiques in New Orleans. The mirror is Biedermeier, German, circa 1830, from Tom Stansbury Antiques.

The bedroom suites were designed as sanctuaries, retreats from the world. Here an eighteenth-century Oushak sets the tone for the room. The curtains are hand-woven and hand-dyed silk from Namay Samay, which also made the fabric for the bed skirt and the coverlet on the bed. A printed velvet fortuny cover found at Robert Kime in London dresses the bed, rich and warm for cool nights.

All of the furniture in this bedroom has a lively history. The rare Tudor table in front of the window dates from about 1580 and still has traces of its original red oxide paint. The massive stop-fluted ionic columns support a frieze of stylized flowers and scrolls. The Irish Chippendale bedside table dates from about 1760, and the nineteenth-century Scottish barley twist long bookcase was fresh from a Scottish baronial estate.

Andy Gibbs, of Blank Canvas Antiques in Ross-on-Wye, supplied the posts and cornice of the four-poster bed. Bruce Isaac Furniture, an English specialist furniture restorer, built the bed with the antique elements, as handsome old beds rarely come in king size.

The Italian eighteenth-century walnut doors were added where there had been none to separate the bedroom from the bathroom. They were reclaimed from a Tuscan Villa that had fallen into disrepair. All of the hallways and passages in the house have been filled with bookcases, as the owners have an interesting and eclectic taste in books and there is no separate space in the house for a large library. Kate and Odom feel that rows and rows of books add character to a house and an insight into the inhabitants' personalities.

Kate and Odom designed the circular bookcases in the tiny turret library, having them painted and adding the molding and details to a previously characterless space.

The Italian Grand Tour table with its kinetic giltwood dolphin base and specimen marble table is Italian, circa 1820. The delicate parcel-gilt chairs are also Italian, early nineteenth century. The curtain fabric is from Fermoie in England.

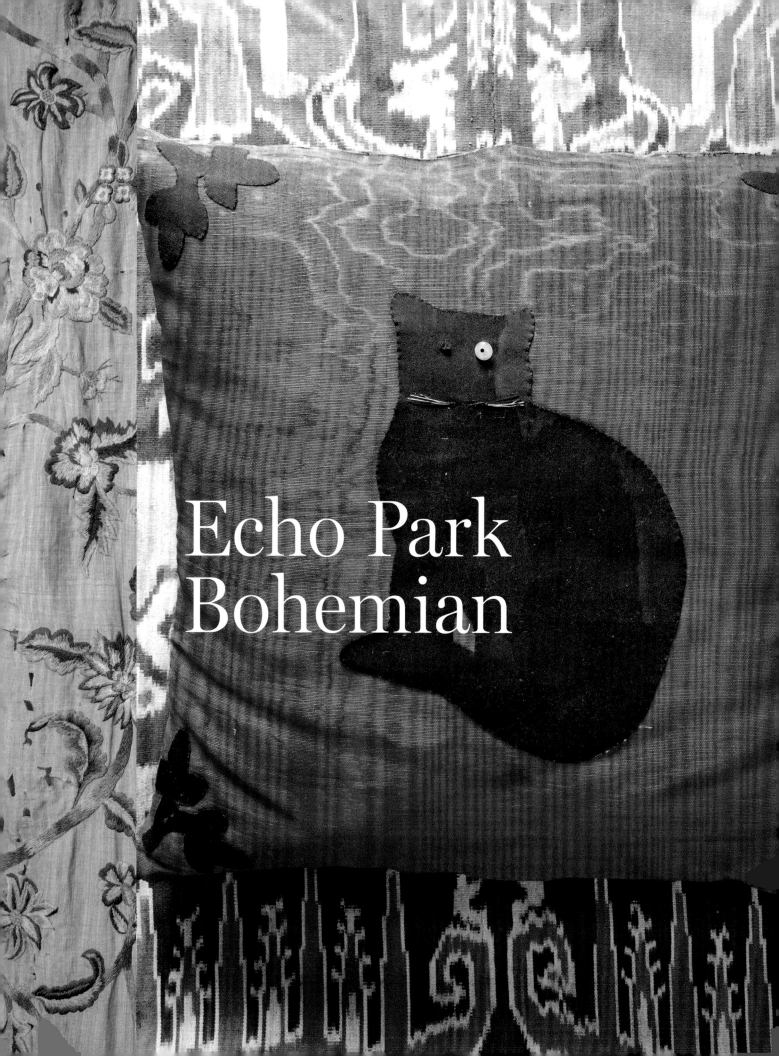

Echo Park
Bohemian

Angelino Heights, an historic neighborhood rich with beautifully restored landmark Victorian mansions dating back to 1886, is an anomaly in Los Angeles. The past is revered. Tangles of freeways and rush hour are distant and forgotten here. Elegant and sedate tree-lined streets, some still with traces of old trolley lines, feel securely protected, even though they now border style-resonant and very cool Echo Park.

Set within this array of architectural beauty is the ultra-private Angelino Heights retreat of Laurel Myers, a longtime and beloved associate of Stamps & Stamps, and her husband, Yiorgos Tagaras, an importer of luxurious Greek delicacies, including Greek olive oils from his family's estate on the hillsides surrounding Corinth.

The couple's 1904 Craftsman residence stands back from the neat sidewalk, hidden and intriguing. Entry is through a free-form vegetable garden, fragrant with herbs and flowers, a paradise for butterflies and bees. Surrounding the house are fruit-producing trees, with a year-round bounty of heirloom apples, pomegranates, figs, mulberries, lemons, limes, and kumquats.

A quick leap up ten stone stairs leads to the wood-framed porch of their residence, its shingles and clapboard true to the Craftsman ideals. Magenta-throated bright blue trumpets of morning glories and a rich crimson bougainvillea intertwine around the posts. Passionflowers with periwinkle and green and white blossoms festoon the eaves. From the porch, city views of nearby downtown Los Angeles appear. On clear nights, silver skyscrapers are lit in cinematic relief from the western sun.

The house, originally a guesthouse for an adjacent mansion, was built at a time when Arts & Crafts architecture was flourishing in many neighborhoods of old Los Angeles. Craft, quality materials, and individuality were signatures of these bungalows and grand houses.

Here in the domain of Laurel and Yiorgos, rooms are beautifully proportioned and full of light and air. The couple's lifelong global collections enrich every room. Laurel studied art and design in Florence during college and then traveled throughout Europe, doing a deep dive into old paintings, textiles, and antiques. After graduating, she joined the staff of Stamps & Stamps, traveling with Kate to England, Europe, and Turkey in search of paintings, antiques, and rare decorative elements for specific projects. Along the way she picked up the quirky and elegant treasures now in her home.

"I'm always looking for slightly mysterious antiques and art with character and humor and style that are not popular and are ignored," says Laurel. Seeking out eccentric pieces with no precise provenance or famous name, she is also alert to artistry and rarity. Willing to accept signs of wear, she unearths bargains at auctions, in aristocratic attics, and even from prestigious specialists.

Yiorgos, who travels throughout the Peloponnesus and Greek islands with Laurel and keeps his eyes open for icons and paintings, has amassed an impressive and delightful collection of ships in bottles. These miraculous worlds-under-glass add luster and delight in every room.

Best of all, there's also a sunny sheltered terrace that they use in all seasons for breakfast and lunch, and especially for weekend entertaining. It's here that family and friends gather to taste the best of Greek delicacies, and to linger on into the night surrounded by the lovely garden.

Opposite: In the living room a faded pomegranate silk velvet adds luster and charm to the elegant carved Venetian sofa, found at auction in San Francisco. Antique needlework joins Fortuny pillows filled with European down. Above the sofa is a compelling Mannerist painting of religious figures, Italian seventeenth century. Laurel's collection is marvelously eclectic and vivid, and all pieces are notable for their craftsmanship, rarity, humor, and attitude. Holding stacks of favorite art, design, and travel books, the circular copper-banded table with a rare richly colored rosewood top by Steen Ostergaard for Poul Cadovius is one of the only great twentieth-century classics in the residence. Pride of place is given to one of Tagaras's ship-in-bottle models, of turquoise glass with

a miniature schooner inside. More than thirty of these handmade marvels, a tribute to his sea-faring Greek heritage, are visible in each room.

Above: The small Indian wooden peacock figure, carved and gilded, is here used as an impromptu table. A large antique French library chair is draped with ikats from Istanbul and a dark green and yellow suzani from Uzbekistan. "Fabrics made in traditional styles that are time-intensive and require dazzling feats of design and adherence to old techniques and hues and fibers always draw my complete attention," Laurel says. "Handcrafted textiles bring warm and rich textures to our rooms. I am grateful to the families and devoted artisans who create them."

Above and opposite: In the study stands a striking Scottish mahogany secretaire, with elegant glass-paneled doors, circa 1840. The brass inlaid and delicately carved pair of side chairs date from around 1815. A panel of embroidered silk from Kos hangs above one of the chairs. Safari chairs by Kaare Klint have goatskin cushions with a leopard-printed pattern. Curtains are in Schumacher's "Pyne Hollyhock" chintz.

Following pages: On the table stands a nineteenth-century German wood filigree ornament, an ornate pocket watch holder, and a clock tower for a grand timepiece.

The eccentric hand-carved ebonized Anglo-Colonial sofa has a dramatically carved rooster head and cockscomb arms.

William Blake: Dante's *Divine Comedy*

Above and opposite: In the dining room, an eighteenth-century mythological English painting, acquired for its compelling oddity, depicts Chronos casting spells with attendant cheeky cherubs. Laurel entertains frequently and has the loveliest linens, some of which were embroidered by her mother-in-law, Eleni. The Dutch mahogany linen press, with beautiful carvings and panels, holds stacks of them. The dining table is dressed with an eighteenth-century golden Italian silk velvet coverlet, topped with a lace and cutwork and crochet tablecloth. On the walls are English crewelwork panels originally from the residence of Andrew Lloyd Webber. On the slipcovered sofa is a Greek hand-woven rag rug.

Following pages: In a corner of the dining room is a Mediterranean collection of religious ephemera. An English jardiniere adorned with pinecones and twigs was repurposed into a decorative bar.

Previous pages: The superbly carved bed is eighteenth-century Portuguese, dressed with family heirloom linen sheets and pillowcases with a Portuguese matelassé cover for texture. The eighteenth-century Castello Branco textile, too fragile for everyday use, hangs on the wall above the bed. The hand-made quilt, made from Spitalfields' silk and bound in eighteenth-century damask, that sits at the foot of the bed is from Kate's favorite textile dealer, Peta Smyth, in London. The Chinoiserie dressing table is from the contents of a very grand English duchess's house. The carpet is 1920s French in exquisite tones of pink.

Opposite and above: In the kitchen, a nineteenth-century Ottoman cypress kavakluk, originally used as a turban cabinet, houses Laurel's immense collection of cookbooks, new and vintage. Tacked to the side of the kavakluk are Yiorgos's and Laurel's collection of ex-votos.

Honeysuckle sends waves of intense perfume over the terrace. Laurel and Yiorgos's dining room and terrace can seat fifteen to twenty people for large feasts. Silk floss trees bower over the garden and jasmine scents the air. Pots full of roses, kale, herbs, kumquats, and abutilon flourish, combining beauty and practicality.

The couple spend most of their weekends entertaining here, inviting friends and family to enjoy the Tagaras

bottarga from Messolonghi and truffles foraged in the Peloponnese and Thessaloniki. There are cheeses made by nuns in Corinth, honey from Kythera, and sea salt harvested in the Mani. The painted tin tray is in traditional patterns from Kea, in the Aegean near Athens.

"We have a small bungalow and garden, but we use every inch," says Myers. "In winter we light the garden fire, and it's very cozy."

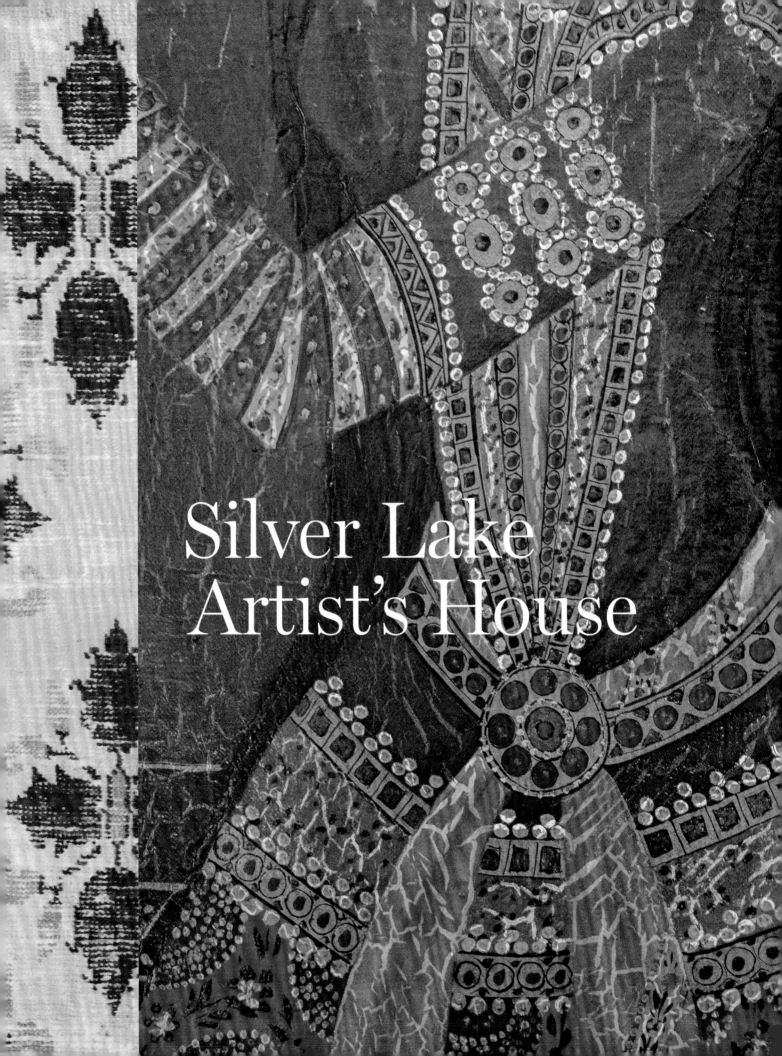

Silver Lake Artist's House

Silver Lake, in central Los Angeles, is surrounded by the intriguingly named and popular neighborhoods of Echo Park, Los Feliz, Angelino Heights, and Elysian Heights. Silver Lake is also known historically as a favorite hillside haven for designers and artists. Many midcentury houses that populate its hills were designed by the likes of Richard Neutra, Rudolf Schindler, John Lautner, and Frank Lloyd Wright among others.

The owners of this recent renovation by Stamps & Stamps are artists and passionate about the decorative arts. Color and textile and pattern and detail ornament each room. The couple commissioned Stamps & Stamps to redesign their hillside cottage from the 1930s to add an extra floor, and to enrich every room with art and antiques.

Odom consolidated three rooms into the kitchen, and elsewhere added a domed entrance hall and created a new family room and terrace. The entire third floor is new, and Odom's alterations are seamless. The house is now a practical, functional four-bedroom house, completely changed without losing any of its character and charm.

Beautiful textiles, antique, rare, and unusual, are the stars of each room. In the sitting room, Kate designed bookcases and banquettes, and added wall hangings like the 1950s suzani worked in saffrons and sapphires. The cushions are a mix of exotic carpet fragments, embroidered textiles, nineteenth-century Fez embroideries from Morocco,

seventeenth-century Isfahan carpet fragments, Chinese brocades, and tribal mirrored vegetable-dyed pieces.

The chandelier is made of blue agate glass shades suspended from a gilded metal oval on simple brass chains. The pyramidal floor lamps were adapted from eighteenth-century Italian altar candlesticks, made of naively marbled dark painted wood. So that the room is not just a simple Moroccan-style pastiche, Kate added in two bold English chairs. One is a George III Gainsborough chair, classic and solid. She slipcovered it in the finely made Nathalie Farman-Farma Décors Barbares fabric. The caned chair is also English, circa 1810.

The family room is at the back of the house and opens onto the lovely Silver Lake landscape. As it is small and the family wanted to have maximum seating, Kate made a comfortable upholstered corner sofa that is slipcovered in a Peter D'Ascoli handmade printed linen in rich cerise, patterned with a paisley design. The throw pillows are full of down and rich with blue, gold, persimmon, and reds. There are Uzbek ikats and Italian embroideries, Indian cotton prints, and their glamorous cousins from France. More serious and rare suzanis hang on the walls. A favorite dates from the 1870s and is beautifully embroidered on canary-colored silk. The carpet is a fragment of a Turkish carpet, covered with a pattern of sprigs of flowers, from Robert Kime in London.

The dramatic Silver Lake house rises on a hillside above vivid bougainvillea, aloe, and a collection of succulents. The majestic deodar cedar is almost a century old, a local landmark.

The sitting room features the original painted wood beams; vibrant curtains of rust wool satin from Holland & Sherry and a saffron and red suzani on the wall inject bold color and pattern into the décor. A pair of Stamps & Stamps upholstered club chairs are slipcovered in cream brushed canvas. The 1920s Turkish rug floats on natural matting.

Opposite: In the sitting room, a trio of cylinder tables designed by Stamps & Stamps are upholstered in intensely colored and embroidered suzani fabric. The pillows are nineteenth-century Fez embroidery from Peta Smyth in London, and rare carpet fragments from Y & B Bolour in Los Angeles.

Above: The dining room holds a French nineteenth-century refectory table, which has an inset Carrera marble top. It is surrounded by American Gothic chairs of the 1850s in dark mahogany, from Neal Auction Company in New Orleans. They are upholstered with fabric from

London designer and textile specialist Robert Kime. The glazed cabinet with serpentine wooden munitions is Dutch, late eighteenth century, from Tom Stansbury Antiques

Following pages: The custom-made banquette is covered in an artisan-printed cotton from India, by Peter D'Ascoli. The center table is nineteenth century Moroccan, inlaid in an intricate geometric pattern. The cushions are Indian, Moroccan, Indonesian, French, and Turkish, and were found at Penny Worrall in London and at Pat McGann in Los Angeles. The curtains are a classic Braquenié print from Pierre Frey.

Above and opposite: Odom designed the new staircase with a silhouette bannister, along with a new library with bookcases of hand-shaped plaster on the landing. French doors open to a sunny terrace.

Following pages: The master bedroom with its luxurious barrel-vaulted ceiling, sitting room, bath, and terrace are all part of the new addition. The delicately painted and gilded early-nineteenth-century headboard is Portuguese, with ornately carved stylized scrolls and leaves. The curtains are in a luxurious silk print, and the vellum-covered bedside tables are made for the house. The carpet is nineteenth-century Bakhtiari, and the extraordinary Regency center table is circa 1815.

Adjacent to the bedroom is a new arched balcony and terrace that opens to a view of palm and loquat trees and the Santa Monica Mountains in the distance. Odom designed the colonnaded arches with simple pared-down capitals in the Spanish colonial vernacular and configured them to catch the breezes and pull them in from the hilltop.

Opposite: The long galley kitchen has cabinetry and woodwork in different styles. Some have pickets, others have caned fronts and or paneled wood, all surrounded by hand-glazed tiles in a soft yellow. The pantry has a nineteenth-century Moroccan door and the floor's Mexican terra cotta tiles are spliced in half and arranged in an artful basket-weave pattern.

Previous pages: The upstairs sitting room is designed to be multipurpose, for reading, sleeping, and writing at the Gustavian painted desk. The French daybed circa 1840 is dressed with a collection of patchwork quilts, suzanis, and silk embroidered Rabat pillows. The French carpet from 1870 is an Aubusson in the manner of a Bessarabian carpet.

In the bathroom, a pair of marble-topped custom cabinets with nailhead trim flank a painted cabinet made in Algeria. It's signed in Arabic and French by the original studio. It has an elaborate painted and carved cartouche panel with a monogram.

Hancock Park
Grande Dame

H ancock Park is a rather sedate neighborhood located in a grid of palm-shaded streets west of downtown Los Angeles and east of Beverly Hills. It is one of the oldest neighborhoods in the city, built mostly between 1910 and 1940. House-proud residents protect the essential classical character of the area with strongly enforced design approval controls, and it retains much of its original grandeur.

Idealistic from the start, Hancock Park was planned to follow the philosophy of Frederick Law Olmstead's City Beautiful movement, with spacious houses surrounded by a beautifully landscaped park-like setting. Today the neighborhood has a pleasant urban/suburban character with large houses of quiet elegance.

Stamps & Stamps was approached by the cosmopolitan owners of a classical 1930s house, which over time had become a pastiche of French and English details.

"We saw the potential, even though most of its interesting exterior character had been stripped away," said Kate. Odom added a dramatic new treillage portico overlooking the garden to enhance outdoor living and offer a gracious view of the landscape. He also added new neoclassical French detailing on the facade. His goal was to make the best of the existing architecture, and to create a convincing French-style harmony.

Odom notes that in a renovation, he aims to make the best of what is there. "I make a careful assessment and always practice restraint balanced with creativity," he says. "I don't believe in rebuilding or demolishing. It then becomes a costly, time-intensive project, with no added value to the homeowner."

For the interiors, Kate felt it was important to respond to the grand proportions of the rooms without losing the feeling of a family house. "We decided to use the most beautiful objects and furniture we could find, but to arrange them in a way that was inviting and human, personal, and meant for a lifetime of living for this family," says Kate.

The house was originally quite dark, with deep-walnut stained floors, and the family wanted a light touch, so Kate had the floors bleached and took great inspiration from Scandinavian interiors of the eighteenth and nineteenth centuries. The colors of the interiors are gentle, but carefully planned.

The sitting room's walls are layered in five different glazes including green and umber so they have a rich and luminous effect. The light reflects beautifully through the strata of color, changing as the sun moves across the room. The upholstered furniture is covered in patterns and colors in subtle hues, all set on richly textured Waveney traditional rush matting.

T he large-scale paintings and textiles hanging on the walls are the perfect counterpoint in color and culture to the luxurious European furniture. A seventeenth-century hand-embroidered panel from India, a palampore from the end of the eighteenth century, and a rare early suzani, all bought from Peta Smyth Antique Textiles in London, accompany a pair of colonial South American portraits of bishops, in gilded frames, bought at Neal Auction in New Orleans.

Above: In the Hancock Park sitting room, Stamps & Stamps custom-designed the dramatic and bold "Sloop" chair, which is slip-covered with a Lee Jofa hand-blocked floral chintz. The sitting room is large, so the overscale chair and print are ideal.

"This chintz is made in a very traditional style, all by hand, and even the wood blocks are hand-carved to give a beautifully crafted look," says Kate. "The roses and leaves and twigs look particularly beautiful but unexpected in Los Angeles. The colors, muted. I love them."

Opposite: The stairway has a scrolled iron balustrade, painted white, that moves gracefully up and across the landing. A Swedish eighteenth-century settee painted greenish-gray has traditional cream and beige ticking. Pillows are in bourette de soie and an Italian brocade. The wall hanging in French silk and silver thread is from Peta Smyth, London.

Above: The English eighteenth-century hand-carved pine mantel, found by Kate in London, is exquisite, in the tradition of Grinling Gibbons and Matthias Lock.

Opposite: For the sitting room, Kate ordered Waveney Rush handwoven matting. "It's beautiful underfoot, soft and thick, and all natural," says Kate. "I grew to love it when visiting English country houses. The concept is centuries old in England, and it works wonderfully in Los Angeles as well."

Rush matting is crafted in strips from hand-harvested natural bulrushes that grow on river banks. These woven strips are joined to make rugs, which are bound neatly on all sides. When the custom rugs arrive, fresh, they are a pale green color, and they fade over months to a soft neutral wheat tone. They smell faintly grassy, of the earth and of the sea.

The eighteenth-century Swedish chair at left was found at an auction in Copenhagen. Over the mantel is a rare sixteenth-century English oil on canvas landscape.

The sitting room is composed classically, with hand-printed chintz, and a corner banquette slipcovered in a Rose Cumming jacquard weave fabric. Pillows include a collection of bourette de soie antique fabrics and needlepoint. Hexagonal tables designed by Stamps & Stamps were given a Moroccan star treatment with ribbon secured by antique brass nailheads. The wall hanging is Indian palampore. The seating is divided into three separate groups; the first and most often used are arranged at the fireplace, the others in banquettes and club chairs at opposite sides of the room. Almost everything is slipcovered, an essential element to keep a room from feeling formal and staged.

In the dining room, walls are painted a pale green with egg and dart architectural motifs. Décor was influenced by neoclassical Scandinavian rooms of the late eighteenth century that emphasize elegant simplicity and understated materials. Chairs by Christopher Howe are painted in a traditional taupe/gray/green tone. The floor is hand-painted with a semi-transparent glaze in geometric patterns.

Kate custom mixed a multidimensional wall color for the bedroom. Into the pale off-white base color, she added drops of mauve and pink to create a soft, soothing color that turns pink-apricot in the afternoon sun. The four botanical prints are by Robert John Thornton, an English artist.

On the king-size Hästens bed is a cover in an early-twentieth-century damask with silver threads. The skirt and bedhanging are Chelsea Textiles, hand-embroidered with silk in a tracery of vines and flowers. The English nineteenth-century gothic carved corner cabinet is from Ann Koerner in New Orleans.

Above: The Swedish oak secretaire is from the eighteenth century and was found at auction in Copenhagen. It is perfect for note writing and email composing in the early hours, with a cup of tea poured from a tiny Sicilian pot once owned by Sophia Loren. Over the bed hangs a hand-embroidered silk bed curtain from Chelsea Textiles.

Following pages: The Hancock Park loggia overlooks a swimming pool and is perfect for dining al fresco. Odom designed this new structure with bold columns and treillage and an intricately crafted ceiling. The floor was reclaimed from a French château that had been demolished. The painted metal sofa and chairs are by McKinnon and Harris, Richmond, Virginia.

Pasadena Collectors
House

Kate Stamps first met jewelry designer Annie Higgins, founder of the Anabel Higgins Jewelry company, more than two decades ago. Together they've decorated five Higgins family houses in Southern California. Both designer and collector share an enduring love of eighteenth-century English and French antiques, richly detailed and rare antique textiles, beautiful English table settings, and chandeliers with sparkle and eccentric character. Annie is an enthusiastic collaborator, knowledgeable of the creative process.

Recently for Annie and her husband, Chris Higgins, and their children, Kate and Odom Stamps renovated and restyled a classical Cape Code-style house in Pasadena. "Pasadena has a powerful sense of history," says Kate. "This dynamic region has always had grand estates that border the Arroyo Seco and extend for hundreds of acres." The tree-shaded neighborhood around the Higgins house is enriched by landmarked traces of the fin-de-siècle grandees who colonized Pasadena.

The Higgins's residence, designed in 1939, was one of the last built in the pre–World War II boom. It's Cape Cod in inspiration, built on the high point of a ridge on the northern edge of Pasadena. Stamps & Stamps has adapted and improved elements of the house, while retaining its essential classical character.

Odom first reconfigured the interiors and added dormers and a cupola. To give the house refinement and architectural detail it lacked, he and Kate added grace notes like simple surrounds, columns, architraves, and pediments to the doors and doorways on the main floor. In the living room, they added a nineteenth-century English carved pine and gesso mantelpiece. These seemingly small alterations upgraded and dignified the house to make it seem more architecturally distinguished.

Kate had the floors of the sitting room painted in a diagonal checkerboard of cream and warm beige to bring soft reflected light indoors. The geometric pattern is decorative, and the painted wood floor is practical for a family with two beloved dogs. She custom-designed paint for the walls in the sitting room and halls in an uplifting pale blue that keeps the rooms light but not cold.

"The Higgins family have rare Swedish eighteenth-century fauteuils, which make bold silhouettes in the sitting room," says Kate. "They love to entertain, and their sitting room is full of comfort and treasures."

The unusual compound convex églomisé mirror above the fireplace is English, dating from around 1810. It's richly gilded, and the mirror is back-painted in a soft shimmer that was intended to catch and reflect candlelight in the time before electricity.

Most of the antiques here have an august provenance. The faience tray table, which is Swedish, circa 1770, came from Rose Terrace, the Grosse Pointe Farms estate of Anna Dodge. It is beautifully decorated with a hand-painted urn, neoclassical and restrained.

The curtains in the sitting room are simply styled as a neutral counterpoint to the color and pattern and richness of the room. They are a clotted cream color in matte silk, lined and interlined, and trimmed with a simple Samuel & Sons silk fan edge.

In each room, delight is in the details. Using Annie's collections, and orchestrating new finds from London and Istanbul, Kate highlights their intriguing backstories, rare provenances, recherché crafts, beautifully eccentric colors, or complex histories.

Previous pages: The entrance hall is a welcoming juxtaposition of color, silhouette, and history, including panels of Annie's favorite Zuber wallpaper mounted on drywall and framed. A gilded gothic ornamental architectural fragment, possibly from a private chapel, holds a nineteenth-century luster urn from KRB NYC, overflowing with flowers from the garden. The scroll-arm chairs have a kinetic energy, and the miniature French gilded daybed provides a pretty perch.

Opposite and above: In the sitting room, the dynamic geometric pattern of the painted floor adds bold graphic style. The neoclassical parcel-gilt, painted chair, one of a set of four, is Swedish, upholstered with Chanteloup cotton chintz by Le Manach. The gilded table, French circa 1850, is carved with a faux tree trunk and frolicking children and dogs. Next to the sofa, garden roses and a contemporary painting stand on a faience tray-topped ebonized table from Tom Stansbury Antiques. The lamp, late nineteenth century, is a brilliant turquoise opaline glass.

Above the Adam-style English pine mantel is a four-part framing of a convex silvered class mirror. The star of the room is the Stamps & Stamps upholstered chair of a grand scale covered with a tailored but-not-tight slipcover in one of Kate's favorite fabrics, Chanteloup, from Le Manach. "We wanted to keep this fabric as the main print in the room, as it has a bold design that adds movement and excitement to the room," says Kate.

The English club chair is crafted in centuries-old techniques with a hardwood, double-doweled frame, hand webbing, hand-knotted and hand-tied springs, cotton batting, and a natural cotton muslin ticking. The back is tight, with a loose seat cushion. The slipcover is skirted and designed to look loose and relaxed. With its traditional structure, comfort, and durable contraction, the chair is expected to last decades and sail through time as a beloved family heirloom.

Most of Annie Higgins's collection of floral and botanical paintings and embroideries are in this room. Beyond the sofa is Annie's collection of English and French watercolors of flowers. There are French eighteenth-century reverse-painted bouquets, exquisite shadow box embroideries worked in silk and chenille from around 1800, and watercolor paintings by noted botanical artists, as well as English Regency ladies' drawing room pictures executed by gifted and anonymous amateurs from a time when it was important for young women to "paint a little." Each one evokes a different time and place.

Opposite: Part of Annie's collection of Vieux Paris turquoise monogrammed porcelain is arranged on the charming brass-bound English mahogany waterfall bookcase. The monograms are large and decorative and originally announced the nineteenth-century hosts' social standing to all the guests.

Above: The small scallop-backed banquette, which was acquired at auction in Paris, is from the estate of great French antiquaire and interior designer Madeleine Castaing, who had an admired design shop in Paris for decades. The banquette is covered in her signature turquoise silk-linen and bound in a classic Castaing fringed border. "This graceful sofa had been loved and used when we acquired it, but it was perfect, so we simply reupholstered it in the same silk-linen fabric, same style," notes Kate.

Opposite and above: In the dining room, a turquoise French opaline glass chandelier with gilded metal mounts adds a jolt of color. The dining table is covered in a boldly patterned suzani from Azerbaijan in turquoises and pinks. For the walls, Kate mixed a custom paint in rich peach/terracotta, which casts flattering light for dinner parties and is a perfect backdrop for Annie's porcelain collections, which include Wedgwood shell plates, Sèvres coffee cups and saucers, English pink luster from the 1830s, charming transferware and precious Meissen, unified in their varying shades of pink.

Previous pages: The fall-front desk, early American, is a rare version of japanned furniture of the late eighteenth century. The Chinese carpet with its bold blues enlivens the room, and the handmade wallpaper panels are from Mauny.

Part of Annie's Wedgwood Pink Pearlware Nautilus dessert service frames an eighteenth-century botanical watercolor.

Above: The Danish mythological scene oil painting includes trumpeting mermaids, a merman, and a rescued maiden, in allusive watery colors and brushwork.

Opposite: The large silhouettes are of the great-grandparents of Ivor Gurney, the WWI poet and composer, and were found at the Lacquer Chest in London.

Opposite: In the sunroom, everything is bright and color-ful. The eight-foot-long wicker sofa, a family heirloom, is covered with pieced and paneled antique fabrics in a rich collage. The pillows include a striking ikat. The pair of octagonal tables is nineteenth-century Syrian. The tufted chair is upholstered in the French style, with a panel of Prelle silk brocade.

Above: A French tufted chaise longue is covered in an ikat-patterned linen weave by Nicholas Herbert. The antique cabinet in ebony and ivory is Italian. The oil paintings of birds on boards are Italian, late eighteenth century.

The landing, a newly created space, holds impressive collections of silhouettes and portraits. It's a comfortable reading nook with two English Regency chairs and well-stocked bookcases. The turquoise and pink of the framed panels of Mauny wallpaper give strong color and a wonderful organizing backdrop to the silhouettes. Most of Annie's silhouettes are cut from paper, some embellished with grisaille shadow or gold highlights, but the gems of her collection are those reverse painted on glass, which are as fragile and rare as they are complicated and artistically demanding. Some of these, especially the ones done between 1770 and 1780 in Denmark and Sweden, are incredibly intricate, with full figures and furniture and draperies rendered in silhouette.

The master bedroom is full of charming works of fine and decorative arts. Above the fireplace is a Dutch needlework panel, stitched in about 1800. The armchair is hand-printed linen by Hazelton House. Across the room, the settee is a family heirloom. It's French, dating from around 1825, with neoclassical carvings typical of the early Empire period. It is covered in a turquoise silk velvet chenille. The four-panel screen behind the settee is Belgian, early eighteenth-century, found at Tom Stansbury Antiques, and it depicts the four seasons in the guise of a gardener performing seasonal tasks.

The carpet is Chinese, from the 1930s, and still retains its rich sapphire jewel tones. The lamps are made from rare eighteenth-century grisaille decoupage vases found at the Lacquer Chest in London.

Above and opposite: Odom added dormers to the upstairs rooms, which created cozy nooks. Here, a collection of engravings of George Washington live above a French 1820s fruitwood daybed upholstered in Le Manach's Mortefontaine, as is the nearby French eighteenth-century fauteuil. The painted Moroccan star-shaped table adds a touch of exoticism.

The bed hangings were originally in the nursery of Lady Elizabeth Bowes-Lyon, who later became the Queen Mother. The cotton damask woven with a pattern of heather flowers is typical of the 1870s. They are set into an Italian parcel gilt and painted crown and draped over the sleigh bed upholstered in La Folie, a fabric from Tissus d'Hélène. Above the bed is a set of water-colored cards from the Victorian card game Happy Families. A favorite painting, an 1880s French oil on canvas of a sleeping girl, hangs above the bookcase.

Following pages: In this bedroom, Kate designed a draped bed out of nineteenth-century French toile decorated with palms. The French provincial wing chair is covered with Pierre Frey cotton. In the adjacent bathroom, the cabinet is from the estate of Bunny Mellon and the vanity has a printed linen skirt by Décors Barbares.

It seldom rains in summer in Southern California, so an Indian cotton dhurrie carpet was confidently selected for the floor of the terrace. The chairs are reproductions of Regency wirework furniture. "Annie loves to entertain in the garden, and her favorite colors, turquoise and pink, are reiterated here," says Kate. The pretty hues were selected for pillows, cushions, tablecloths, the painted umbrella, and the rug.

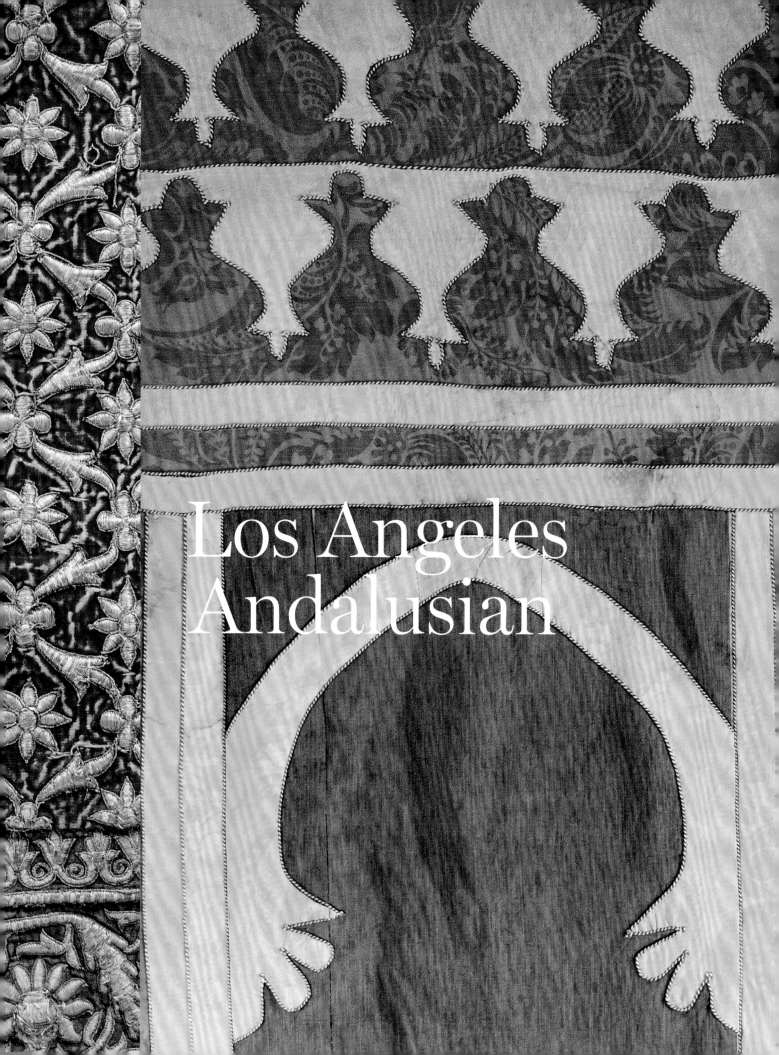

Los Angeles Andalusian

Romantic Andalusian-inflected houses of Tangier and Fez and Marrakech were striking inspirations for the Los Angeles casa Stamps & Stamps redesigned for Craig Brill and Todd Schurko, their urbane clients. This traditional Spanish house sits on the edge of Beverly Hills in a tree-shaded site, discreetly hidden from the street, rather like a traditional residence in southern Spain.

With Odom and Kate's guidance and collaboration, the residence feels expansive. A boldly graphic nineteenth-century Moroccan gate with peeling layers of blue and mustard paint leads into the garden and quiet courtyard, where the large city slips away and the charming house is revealed. Garden and house intertwine, perfect for a couple who live inside and outside year-round thanks to the benign Los Angeles climate.

Like many of these small Los Angeles houses built in the 1920s, this one had been built without a true entrance hall. Odom started with a new entrance porch to give visitors a first impression of welcome and grace. He added a tall arched window and filled it with a screen of five pointed stars that expands its pattern in shadows on the walls as the sun draws high.

Odom reinforced the Spanish-Moroccan style with authentic materials like tiles, wooden screens, ironwork, and new architectural details. "Our Mediterranean climate and our Spanish Colonial history in California led us to go in that direction stylistically," says Odom. He created a new kitchen and breakfast room and, on the floor above, a master bathroom, while also adding detail throughout the house and linking it more completely with the garden. Todd and Craig, who founded Los Angeles-based Dogsport, a canine adventure company that takes clients' dogs hiking in canyons or to frolic at a remote beach, are also very talented craftsmen. They designed and installed some of the house's plasterwork as well as the fine tile and mosaic work, including the Moroccan tile in the kitchen and the intricate pebble mosaic starburst in the floor of the master bathroom, guided by Odom and Kate.

Craig and Todd are enthusiastic travelers who have a great fondness for southern Spain and Morocco. After wide-ranging trips in the region they've returned with a superb collection of traditional blue and white pottery, dramatic lighting, tiles, lanterns, handmade carpets and textiles, and rare and antique objects that enhance each room. Much of their fine artwork was left to them by a dear friend, and Kate helped them seek out many unusual and distinctive antiques that now form the basis of their collection.

"We were looking for a mix of interesting pieces that combine elements of many different cultures, and we found them in London, Paris, and in the attic auctions of noble houses in Germany," says Kate.

Previous pages: This scrolled iron gate leads to a quiet citrus-scented garden with a central fountain. Hanging next to the front entrance is a Moroccan lantern of pierced tin and multicolored glass. When the wooden door is open, the newly created entry hall benefits from an intricate wooden screen to modulate the afternoon sun.

Above and opposite: An exuberant Chefchaouen blue paint frames the arched doorways and windows of the sitting

room to dramatic effect. Among the treasures is a pair of Moroccan carved wood chairs inlaid with camel bone and mother-of-pearl. Above the fireplace, original to the house, stands a silk-screen Picasso portrait. The Tunisian daybed is upholstered with a Moroccan carpet covered with an alpaca throw. There's a German, octagonal ebonized wood table with a banquette upholstered in antique embroidered brocade and damask on silk velvet.

Above and opposite: Sunflowers from the garden stand on the German octagonal table topped with favorite books. The banquette, acquired by Kate at a Sotheby's auction of a noble European family's attic treasures, retains its original wool lattice fringe. At right, the French leather club chair, from the 1930s, has a new silk ikat cushion.

Following pages: A Greek olive oil urn flanks the entry to the dining room. Hanging over the dining table, the painting on silk by Edward J. Brown is a protest against the brutality of bullfighting. The Spanish chairs have tooled leather seats and backs. The refectory table, eighteenth century, is also Spanish.

In the breakfast room, a nineteenth-century Moroccan lattice table, carved and inset with mother-of-pearl, serves as a plinth for books on art, design, and cooking. Odom designed the kitchen, with lattice doors in oak. The pointed arches of the niches were inspired by traditional Moorish patterns and apertures seen at Topkapi Palace in Istanbul. Classical square Mexican terra cotta tiles were cut and spliced and set in a herringbone pattern for an authentic style.

In the kitchen, a large antique stone trough sink has a surround of limestone. Cabinet doors, drawers, and plate racks are unfinished oak with a light stain. The nine-foot-long banquette in the breakfast room is covered with a vivid collection of tribal weavings collected on many travels. Pillows were crafted from old saddlebags, antique suzanis, and rug fragments. The chandelier is French.

In the large bedroom, the wall was decorated with a green/brown/terra cotta wall hanging. It's an early Moroccan velvet example, worn down to the smooth surface and faded from its original vivid jewel tones. It contrasts with the gilded brocade of the heavily embroidered Indian bedcover. The textiles are from Charles Jacobsen. A flotilla of pillows consists of an international collection of Turkmen carpet fragments and French silk velvet. At the side of the bed is an improvised table of a terra cotta urn with a mosaic tile top in a peacock pattern.

Odom designed the bathroom layout, and the owners perfected the materials, floors, and walls, which are Moroccan-style burnished integral plaster. The French copper tub sits between two glass cabinets, one of thick, pale green colored glass, which houses the shower, the other of etched glass which obscures the water closet.

The washstands sit opposite each other at the ends of the room, each created with a Turkish marble basin standing on a Carrera marble top. A Moroccan mirror hangs above. This is one of Odom's favorite bathroom designs, perfectly balanced and symmetrical.

After the work was finished on the main house, Odom designed the pool, outdoor entertaining space, and kitchen. It has quiet corners, perfect for two to dine al fresco, while the garden/pool/terrace has welcomed as many as two hundred guests for a quiet summer evening fundraiser.

The garden that surrounds the area is a simple rectangle in its plan, bounded by a tall hedge of ficus. On each end are hand-wrought iron gates inspired by an elaborate design by architect George Washington Smith for an estate in Montecito.

226

After dinner at the long table, a movie screen is raised in the garden and friends gather on steamer chairs and pillows to view classic films. It's the perfect Los Angeles urban experience, private and glamorous, beneath the stars. Brill is an expert cook, and the pizzas that emerge from the outdoor oven are delicious. The Mexican Talavera tiles are made by hand, colored in Todd and Craig's favorite Yves Klein blue and saffron, the perfect counterpoint to the Mediterranean hue of the swimming pool and the emerald of the enclosing hedges.

ARCHITECTURE AND STYLE WISDOM

From Odom and Kate Stamps

Kate and Odom Stamps founded Stamps & Stamps in 1991. For most of their projects, Odom shapes the architecture and Kate designs the interiors. Together they have created hundreds of highly individual houses and interiors around the world. Kate has designed and launched collections of furniture and fabrics, and created rooms of lasting beauty and inspiration. Odom works in a broad range of styles, always seeking authenticity and integrity in his architecture.

Odom Stamps on Architecture

Consider the context. Study the site, the location, the microclimate, and "the spirit of the place" before starting a project. For example, for a renovation or new architecture, learn the history and "social landscape" and ethos of a location. Elaborate architecture would be inappropriate for a simple Cape Cod cottage. Don't put a desert garden in front of a Georgian house. The dissonance will distract. But for interiors, do have a sense of fun and mix things up.

Authenticity and architectural integrity are essential. In South Pasadena we are surrounded by handsome historic residences. Houses should have a timeless, solid, and inspiring quality to make them interesting, warm, and comfortable for years to come. Proportion and detail, scale and suitability, grace and lack of pretension are words to live by. Integrity of materials, functional design, appropriateness, and beauty are fundamental building blocks. When the vision is all-encompassing and the broad strokes and details suit the spirit of the place, a rich sense of humanity and charm will inhabit a house.

There are inexpensive solutions for floors. When we were younger and just starting out, we covered the floors in our studios with seagrass matting, which is a flat weave in a natural light buff color. It's practical and feels comfortable underfoot, and it's very durable. Later we converted our studios to new

purposes; we installed wide-plank oak flooring to create a classic and more permanent feeling. We also used simple Mexican terra cotta tiles in kitchens and bathrooms. You can be stylish, whatever your means.

Our garden was "eco" three decades ago. We are blessed with enough land to create gardenscapes that change with the season. We have planted many trees on our site. They have thrived. Shade from our century-old carobs and oaks keep our house cool all summer. Our gardens are entirely on drip irrigation. Our pathways are composed of pervious sand set with broken concrete slabs and bricks that I get dropped off whenever there is demolition on one of our projects. These construction cast-offs are free, and they are the ultimate in green recycling.

Kate and I work very closely together so that architecture and interior design are harmonious. Sometimes architecture doesn't start out with good bones; it is essential to work a little magic with the incorporation of things like antique chimney pieces and reclaimed tile for floors, or beautiful wooden doors to replace hollow ones. Simple additions of stained and waxed terra cotta tiles cut into rectangles and laid in interesting patterns add a level of authentic detail. Dated dark stained wood floors have been painted in checkerboard and more elaborate patterns and can change a room from the ground up.

The addition of a simple cornice in a room can transform a space. Ceilings can be raised and track lighting removed, pilasters or paneling added. Color and pattern can help to dematerialize the walls in an undistinguished room. If a substantial framework of architecture is completely lacking, we often find very interesting, strongly architectural pieces of furniture to shape the room. Bookcases and large cabinets are most effective for this purpose.

Kate Stamps on Interiors, Style, Gardens

Creating a comfortable and practical house starts with consideration of function and emotion. That results in an inviting kitchen for a child returning from school, the well-laid table that delights a friend, the quiet spot with a comfortable chair surrounded by books. Thoughtful planning engenders a bedroom that encourages pleasant dreams. Rooms provide the visual background of our times and those of our families. If they can be warm and welcoming, interesting and charming, they will enrich everyone's lives.

Not everything should be perfect. Mended porcelain, frayed curtains, gently sun-faded wood bowls, or chipped plates all add to a feeling of softness and ease. I love my eighteenth-century German damask tablecloths with royal monograms. They're elegant. And in my bedroom, I use simple bed linens from Ikea as children, dogs, cats, and birds have all been known to pile on my bed. The marriage of beauty and practicality is one that we all need to find for ourselves. My bedroom curtains have the most exquisite Prelle striped silk taffeta dress panels, but the draw curtains are plain lampshade silk that has been replaced several times after spills. This mix of the poetic and the prosaic keeps the rooms lively and not oppressive, rooms that are meant to be enjoyed and not just impress.

Rooms come alive with great upholstery. Beautiful well-proportioned sofas and chairs add harmony and formal structure. Well-made soft seating gives an instant feeling of welcome, an invitation to sit. A good chaise or settee can be a place for conversation, a spot for reading and repose, a napping place beside the fire on a Sunday afternoon. A beautiful chair, carefully crafted, can be your friend for life, following you from house to house. The perfect sofa makes everyday life better.

A house and its decoration can make peoples' lives richer and more interesting. By surrounding yourself with things that have character and soul, your environment becomes a kind of stimulant, and also a bearer of comfort, both physical and psychic. The building up, layer-by-layer, of collections, personally significant things, and beautiful objects into an environment that educates and soothes can be a lifetime project and will consequently achieve a personal, timeless style, a satisfying permanence.

Avoid "rules" and tired design concepts. Instead look for fresh and personal harmonies and balance. Never match or follow a formula. I always avoid trends and current passions or fashion, and the result is timeless style. Don't be afraid to use strong color or to layer pattern, just keep them in balance.

Keep your interiors personal and interesting. A hotel room may seem enticing and comfortable, and full of great ideas. But even when well designed, it is an impersonal, transitory pleasure, not a home.

Like Nancy Lancaster, I'm "agin' decoratin'," meaning that real creativity is much more than selecting pre-planned matching fabrics or coordinating patterns. Any design theme or scheme you can easily name (French country, California cool, loft, Southwest, "Southern") should be avoided. Trends come and go. Do what you love.

Using print fabrics that are pre-designed to "coordinate" is not decorating. It's not even furnishing. It's essential to take a much more individual, original, and personal design direction. Please refrain from going through a process (planned by some fabric companies) to select two solid fabrics, one stripe, one large pattern, and one small figured pattern to make a room wonderful.

Gather ideas from a favorite painting, a wallpaper, porcelain, photography, and then expand the vision. Making a room beautiful is less about new fabric and style of the curtains than you think. It is about creating the right background and architecture first, with doors and windows in proportion, floors right, and ceiling perfect. Then consider furniture and placement. And plan a more eclectic approach with fabrics, including some antique textiles and tribal rugs or hand-painted wallpaper panels, and create thoughtful contrasts and juxtapositions.

Mine the best inspiration from the past, in books and magazines and image sites, but keep the knowledge as a background in your internal creative library. Don't copy. Look at inspiring rooms for one or two ideas. Define your own authentic style, and be true to yourself. Make every room different and individual. Don't fall back on just the tried and true in your decorating past. Always keep it fresh, perhaps even eccentric, certainly personal.

Flow is important. Always look at a house as a whole and keep all of the relationships between rooms in mind as you plan their uses and decoration. Think of color associations, stylistic consonance, and easy function. Together they make a house feel a coherent whole.

Daily pleasure. Find a way to make every room ideal for everyday enjoyment. To get more use from every room, for example, put a reading nook in the entrance hall, a game table in your sitting room, a library in your dining room, or a tiny breakfast table in your library. If you can use your rooms in many ways, you will use them more often. Don't limit the dining room to the occasional formal dinner party. Rethink and change rooms–perhaps to be a new setting for children's projects, informal gatherings, cocktails, and weekend family gatherings.

Planning a dinner party. Determine the number of people you are likely to have at a dinner party, then make sure you have the same number of seats in a place to gather (for example, the sitting room) before and after the meal. If you are lucky enough to have one room for drinks and conversation before supper and another for coffee after the meal, that is lovely, and your house accommodates the movable feast.

Books furnish a house. Books add soul and reassurance and pleasure. A house or apartment without books is a house without heart. Find the subjects that interest you, and the writers with whom you fall in love, then start collecting and reading. Some of my favorite books have been found in London market stalls, New York specialty bookstores, literary festivals, house clearances, and small-town sidewalk sales as well as great antiquarian booksellers like Sotheran's in Piccadilly. Some are bought at my local booksellers and more are ordered from renowned shops like John Sandoe and Heywood Hill. Still others are acquired at author book signings, and more are scavenged online. Most of the volumes are hardcover, and I love beautiful bindings and signed first editions whenever I can find them. I keep second, softcover copies of my best-loved works tucked behind the hardbound editions so I can safely reread them in the bath. Each one is really a friend, and a portal into another world.

Rooms must smell marvelous. One or two of my favorite rose geranium–scented candles are lit in my house wherever I'm there. The floral, leafy perfume is clean, like the scent of the garden itself. When you use a single fragrance, it will become your house's signature, and your family and visitors will all associate that aroma with you and the pleasant memories you create for them in your home. There

are other ways to add a hauntingly beautiful redolence to your rooms. Fresh lavender and roses from the garden arranged in your favorite cream-ware vase along with rosemary and mint, boughs of orange blossoms in Regency baskets, citrus fruits stuck with cloves piled high in an Imari compote, and magnolia blossoms strewn on the chimneypiece are all splendid for their scent. Fresh milled soaps from Caswell-Massey, who have been making their gorgeous products since 1752, are piled high in shell-work baskets in my bathrooms, freshening the air with their clean, natural perfume.

Antiques add personality and style. Look for chairs and tables and sofas with character. Find lamps that are made from antique objects. Mix ornaments and furniture from different eras, disparate countries and towns, and varied styles in your rooms. The aim is not to match anything or everything. The mélange keeps rooms interesting and full of life.

The art of juxtaposition. The great English deco-rator John Fowler created rooms of great harmony and beauty. With a sympathetic mix of classical and updated pieces from around the world and over the centuries, he made memorable rooms that with-stand the test of time. The rare and the humble, the charming and the fine, all sit comfortably in his spaces. He and Nancy Lancaster made houses that feel inevitable, as if they have always been there. I believe that extraordinary things can be used in a room without making it feel stiff and museum-like, but a thoughtful montage is essential. Rooms are meant to be lived in and should not be designed just to impress. Pretentious interiors are universally boring, but beautiful spaces thoughtfully composed of lovely things are both soothing and stimulating.

Signs of lives well lived. Patina and the gentle wear of antiques keep a house from looking new and over-decorated. I search for quality and craftsmanship in antiques, and love the look of age and time. Pieces should live well together, friendly and harmonious in their setting. A faded carpet, slightly tattered antique textiles, stacks of well-read books, all make a room feel comfortable. A spot where the dog has chewed or where the cat has clawed are a part of life. Small imperfections will make very fine things more affordable and more human in a room and instantly remove stiffness and formality.

Pets with style. Make a place for your pets on sofas and chairs with a washable Indian Kantha quilt, if your animals are indoor/outdoor like mine. A washable blanket or pillow for beloved pets can be part of design. Soul and humanity in a room come from a welcoming spirit.

Group your collections. Hanging fifty fascinating silhouettes in a group together will be so much more compelling than sprinkling them throughout the house. Arrange all of your silver-framed family photos on one big table in a corner. They will live happily together there, regardless of how well in life they managed Thanksgiving dinner. Collections should be carefully edited, selected, and curated. I like exquisite objects and gilded and jewel-encrusted boxes that catch the light and dazzle. Charming simple groups of Regency straw workboxes or quillwork tea caddies thrill me more. Remember the strength of repetition. Have courage in your convictions and design a wall with your entire gallery of watercolors or photography or children's art.

Quality endures. Always buy the best examples of the things you have chosen to collect; they will bring great pleasure. I propose never buying a mediocre piece with the plan to "trade up." You may end up living with that run-of-the-mill piece for a long time. Wait to find the perfect thing, then snap it up. Patience has its rewards.

At ease. Comfort. Always have plenty of comfortable sofas and chairs in a room. They will dependably prevent a room from looking too stiff or formal. Don't overload the sofas with too many pillows, just enough to allow a guest to sit comfortably. Balance the number of skirts and legs in the room. Some chairs are appealing with a short skirt, others need to be covered with a voluminous gather to the floor.

I often start with floors. I select carpets and rugs with great care. I look for fine weaving, color, authenticity, sometimes an eccentric pattern, and certainly signs of expert craftsmanship. I also love mellow, faded, and worn rugs. And sometimes I select a carpet I like, knowing that it is not really big enough for the room. I make it work by putting down a bound seagrass or rush matting in the ideal size, then I place the favorite rug on top. The eye accepts the proportions of the matting, and the antique piece is framed by the neutral color and texture of the natural material. An Oushak or a Persian Polonaise that's a little threadbare is a wonderful thing. They are truly works of art, and their gentle refinement can transform a space.

The beauty of flowers. A room without flowers or a tree or a plant looks rather unfinished to me. Fresh flowers lift a room and make it feel you have paid attention to every detail. Something green and alive brings the garden inside and reinforces our attachment to the natural world. Branches of leaves and spring blooms on a center table, bouquets of roses placed where their scent will astound, a terracotta ale jug stuffed with red-veined Swiss chard and velvety artichoke and scented myrtle leaves, or even baskets with masses of dried hydrangeas should be everywhere. Flowers do not have to be difficult to arrange, and almost anything from the garden or roadside or market can be made marvelous. The vegetable garden is one of the best places to search for all the elements that will make your bouquets strongly architectural, for the worm-eaten glaucous cabbage leaves and the saucer-sized vines of nasturtiums and the prickly, spotted squash foliage are all otherworldly and unexpected. I love their boldness, and this approach can result in the best arrangements I can think of. But a nosegay of lilies or pink tulips from the corner store can be glorious, too. The easiest thing is to take an open-necked container, cut in one stroke a big bunch of a single kind of flower, and drop it in, and you are done.

A rose by any other name. I adore single flowers placed strategically. A perfect pale pink garden rose with pretty leaves in a French nineteenth-century

Champagne flute is perfection. Scented geranium plants trailing their rose perfume from a terracotta basketweave pot can just be lugged in from the garden. I love to see their long pliable branches tumbling over a table edge or hanging on little hooks around a window frame. Annabelle hydrangea flowers dried at their moment of sharpest green add their ethereal pale color and will last in vases for months. Flower branches and berries and autumn leaves look handsome in a large Mason's ironstone pitcher and bring the seasons indoors.

A love of textiles. I have had a lifelong obsession with beautiful fabrics of all kinds. Antique textiles go in virtually every room I decorate, because they always provide a punch, an individual statement that takes decorating from the generic and ordinary to something more imaginative and interesting. These fabrics, like the Anatolian Bokhca wall hanging in the Octagon in Bell Cottage are as much art as craft. A Turkish wall hanging, bought from Şeref Özen in Istanbul, is hand block printed and then hand painted, and probably done in the 1920s. Rare eighteenth-century Turkish çatma cushions are delicate and very hard to come by these days, as their silk-wrapped threads don't hold up to the ravages of time very well.

Fabrics for the perfect finish. In Bell Cottage, a fine square wool paisley shawl, printed in France in the 1830s, is a perfect throw across the back of the desk chair, bringing color and a subtle suggestion of the lives of women who lived in the worlds we know through George Eliot or Anthony Trollope. In the sitting room, the suzani that is folded at the end of the daybed is Samarkand, from the 1940s, and travels from bed to table, just as lovely as a bedcover as it is a tablecloth. It adds an element of exoticism to the room, a little of a romantic vision of distant lands and travels.

Garden views. For Bell Cottage, hidden in our garden, I planted privacy and a lovely view from the bathroom. Outside the bathroom window I planned an ornamental vegetable garden, which is filled with lavender and herbs, tomatoes, beans, and cucumbers on pyramid frames of bamboo. Several varieties of milkweed are tucked among the beds, and we are rewarded with butterflies drifting past the window as they make their migratory detour to enjoy the plants. The birds love it here, too, in this corner of the garden, making their nests in the ligustrum hedge, which has grown to twelve feet, providing complete privacy and shelter for people and animals alike.

Tabletop Style. I have several harlequin sets of glasses, which I use to set the table or to hand around a cocktail. Some are Swedish, another set is French, and my favorite is a group of English wine glasses, which are not really a set at all. The thing they all have in common is that they are nineteenth century and very simply cut, so when one is broken, as inevitably happens, a similar replacement can be found.

I try to mix in colored glass on my tables, as well. I have a set of cobalt Morgantown glasses left to me by my mother-in-law. They were made in the 1940s and are capacious, made to be used with gusto. On the opposite end of the spectrum, I have collected Bristol green wine glasses of different hues and sizes. They are delicate, fragile, and tiny, and date from the eighteenth century. The color brings a kind of magic to the table, as they shine in the candlelight.

My collections of silver came about in much the same way, except for my service for twelve of the Stamps family silver. It's wonderful for the memories it invokes and is perfect, as it's simple and carries our monogram and goes with absolutely everything. Silver flatware is one of those things that goes in and out of fashion, since it needs a little more care than stainless steel. I am always on the watch for interesting fish sets, dessert sets, and fruit sets, which are usually quite ornate, sometimes extraordinary, and can often be picked up at house sales for a song. Because we often entertain in groups larger than twelve, I started to add to my collections with my favorite style of silver, engine-cut Scandinavian flatware. It too is simple in its overall shape, which is a pointed oval at the base, but the delicate tracery on the surface is like lace, feminine and charming in its detail. I bought my first spoons with gilded bowls at a little corner antique shop in Stockholm many years ago, and I add to the mixed set whenever I find some

more pieces. Most of the pieces date from between 1880 and 1914, because of course the Great War changed everything in Europe.

Blue and white china is another essential element for a well-dressed table. It's one of the best choices for an assembled set of porcelain, because the mix makes it even more interesting. Chinese export from the eighteenth century looks lovely with Spode from the nineteenth century and Isis from the twentieth century. The strong patterns and bold blues look beautiful on white linen or saffron suzanis or Indian hand block printed Kalamkari tablecloths, making them endlessly adaptable to beautiful settings of all styles.

But my favorite dishes are my sets of Creamware. First produced in Staffordshire in the 1750s, a beautiful service was made for Catherine the Great and another for Queen Charlotte, and by the 1780s it became known as Queen's Ware. I love the fine and delicate painting that borders the plates and bowls, as the center of the pieces are usually without ornamentation, better to appreciate the perfect rich clotted cream color that gives the pieces their name. Whole sets sometimes turn up at auction, and I love to collect and use them; their unpretentious elegance always sets a perfect note at the dining table.

A Tea Party. Tea parties are fun because they are so pretty. We can partake in the sitting room, or outdoors on the terrace. I love to use my nineteenth-century English china set decorated with ferns and forget-me-nots or my silver pot along with a harlequin set of beautiful cups and saucers. The food is as lovely as the tea service, with crustless sandwich triangles. Cucumber and mint or smoked salmon with spiced cream cheese seem to satisfy everyone, and it is easy to accommodate vegetarians or vegans. And who can resist little decorated cakes? Tea has its own ceremony and is perfect for a celebration with a single friend or a hundred. Baby showers, engagement parties, retirements, and bon voyages can be good causes for a tea, but all you really need is a heated pot and a pretty cup and saucer to make a party.

Some of my necessities and luxuries for tea:

At least two kinds of tea—one traditional and loose leafed, the other herbal.

Beautiful table linens, and especially embroidered tea napkins, new or vintage. Mixed sets of everything are charming at a tea party, and your guests can choose their favorites.

A decorated cake makes everything feel very dressed up, but a homely loaf of homemade Irish soda bread with fresh butter and jam and tea from a traditional brown pot can be a party in itself.

There should be something savory but not substantial to eat. All the guests will need room for cake!

Cocktail Hour. Cocktail parties are Odom's speciality, and he learned the art of bartending as a child in New Orleans. It may not be politically correct these days, but he knew how to mix a very good drink for his parents' and grandparents' friends by the time he was ten. I think he loved the happy sounds of friendly conversation, and I'm sure he overheard a few secrets he shouldn't have, but those benign childhood memories fuel his great pleasure in entertaining now. He makes several classic New Orleans cocktails, but the Sazerac and the Ramos Gin Fizz are my favorites. Since New Orleans is a place where alcohol is likely to be liberally consumed in social situations from dawn to dusk, there is a drink for every phase of the day. It is no hardship to start out with a Gin Fizz in the morning and have a Sazerac in the hour before dinner. We serve our Ramos Gin Fizzes in tall, stemmed water glasses, and the Sazeracs come in short, fat tumblers.

Classic Sazerac
Ingredients
1 cube sugar
3 ounces rye whiskey
3 drops Herbsaint or absinthe
Garnish: lemon twist

Directions
Chill an old-fashioned glass by filling it with ice and letting it sit while preparing the rest of the drink. In a mixing glass, soak the sugar cube with

Peychaud's bitters and muddle to crush the cube. Add the rye whiskey and stir.

Discard the ice in the chilled glass and rinse it with absinthe by pouring a small amount into the glass, swirling it around, and discarding the liquid.

Pour the whiskey mixture into the absinthe-rinsed glass.

Squeeze the lemon twist over the drink to release the essences and then put the lemon twist on the edge of the glass.

Ramos Gin Fizz
Ingredients
2 oz. gin (London Dry or Old Tom)
1 oz. heavy cream
1 oz. simple syrup
1/2 oz. fresh-squeezed lemon juice
1/2 oz. fresh-squeezed lime juice
1 egg white
3 dashes orange blossom water
1 drop vanilla extract, (optional)
Curl of orange peel

Directions
Combine ingredients and dry shake for 10 seconds without ice.

Add several small-to-medium sized ice cubes and shake hard for several minutes.

Continue shaking as long as you are able and until you can no longer hear the ice inside.

Pour foamy contents into a tall chilled glass and slowly top with soda to rise the head.

Garnish with the orange peel.

I like to have passed hors d'oeuvres, especially when there is a large crowd. They should be one single mouthful and tidy to eat, such as baby tomatoes stuffed with crumbled bacon, grated lettuce, and a little mayonnaise; or a tiny potato, creamy and buttery, with a dab of caviar; a fried oyster with a little dip of sauce; cucumber rounds with crème fraîche; or baked cheese in pastry. I also place small bowls of warm spiced nuts all around the room.

THE IMPORTANCE OF UPHOLSTERY

Kate's Tips for Beautiful Furniture

I'm passionate about quality upholstery. I've studied and worked with the best upholsterers and have learned from them. I've pulled apart the finest antique sofas and chairs by the nineteenth-century maker Howard & Sons to find out why they are the most comfortable pieces ever made. Strong hardwood frames, correctly coiled and set springs, and the correct pitch of seat and back are fundamental; the highest-quality down is also essential.

Sofas and chairs must be comfortable, pleasing to the eye and to the body. For both custom and off-the-floor purchases, it's essential to first try out different styles. Always inspect the innards and materials in the seat cushion and the padding on the arms. Inspect the pitch of the back, the height of the arm, the depth of the seat. Some shapes are firmer and more upright, others are slouchier and softer. This is a matter of personal taste, and trying out many options will help you to discover which is best for you. Sit down. Is the chair truly comfortable? Is the back just right, the height perfect, the back cushion firm enough? Turn the floor model over and inspect the underside.

Skirts are attractive, and so are exposed legs. There should be a good balance of legs and skirts in a room. Some skirts should be full, like a Dior New Look skirt, mixed with others that are sleek and glamorous, like Daisy Fellowes. Some pieces can have exposed wood arms or legs, others need to be fully covered to the floor. I also like tailored skirts with inverted pleats, box pleats, and knife pleats. I love short skirts on chairs and sofas as they can bring a bit of whimsy, like a flounce at the hem of a flapper's skirt, or they can be serious, like a parson's waistcoat. It's good fun to see something unexpected in the upholstery shapes, a little humor in the decoration.

Slipcovers add style and grace to chairs and sofas. They are also practical. Almost all of the chairs and sofas I design are slipcovered unless they have exposed, finished wood frames or wonderfully tufted backs. Slipcovers give a room the look of unselfconscious quality, a careful calibration of informality even when the space is grand. Loose covers are why the most formal drawing rooms in English country houses are not off-putting and stiff. The relaxed personality of a slipcover is a wonderful way to offset more imposing furniture and art. They can also be changed easily for a decorating facelift or for a seasonal change. A cozy dark green cut velvet may feel perfect in the winter, and a cool cotton canvas in palest lime green will better suit a summer's day.

Slipcovers should be well made and elegant, never sloppy. Slipshod slipcovers look careless, and nothing in a beautiful room should look careless. At the same time, they should never be tight, as they will instantly make a room feel overwrought. My direction to everyone making a slipcover is that they should fit like a Savile Row suit, beautifully tailored, precisely crafted. And then imagine that the wearer has lost a size. It still fits. The suit is still perfect, just a little loose. The same attention to detail should be paid to the "clothes" your furniture wears.

Slipcovers should be individually tailored for the chair and the room. A series of overlapping folds in skirt corners or an open or closed box pleat or a ruffle will have very different effects in the room. In my sitting room, there is only one sofa with a skirt, and that sofa has the most carefully pleated flounce possible, each little fold precisely measured so it remains tailored, as opposed to a big, fully gathered skirt. These are subtle distinctions, but they affect the overall look of a room powerfully.

Sofas and chairs do not all have to match; in my rooms they are usually of different styles. The old idea of having a matching "suite" of furniture is not a rule I follow. I don't do sets. When rooms look like thoughtful accumulations assembled over the years, they feel human and approachable, even when the things in them are sumptuous. Upholstered and slip-covered furniture sets the visual cues in a room. It will let you know instantly if the space is congenial or unfriendly. Luxury is not about impressing others with rooms full of pretentious furniture; it is about living beautifully. So the sofas in my rooms are usually of different dimensions and different styles. Some have low arms and others may be tall. Some chairs may be made with tight backs, others will have loose cushions, but everything will be, in its own way, comfortable.

Fully upholstered pieces should be more precisely tailored. An eighteenth-century parcel-gilt bergère made for a palace should not look as if it has fallen on hard times. The pattern must be carefully placed, the cord on tape sewn in without puckers, and the gimp applied as perfectly as it would have been in the original workroom. The execution must be as good as the design and suitable for the room it inhabits.

In the end, it is all about the detail. Thoughtful application of trim and passementerie is essential. A contrasting piping around cushions, or adding a pretty tape to the bottom edge of a skirt, can finish it neatly and completely. Passementerie and tassels, fringe and gimp all have a place in the finish of skirts, cushions, and frames. Considering their appropriateness on the individual piece is important, as is their overall impact on the entire room.

BOUQUETS FROM THE GARDEN

Kate's Tips for Beautiful Flowers

Kate Stamps studied flower arranging when living in London as a young student. She was inspired by the traditional, natural-looking bouquets she saw in country houses and churches and friends' London flats and residences. All the masses of roses and clematis, spring blossoms and daffodils, flowering lime tree branches, quince and cow parsley available from the garden were a great inspiration. For Kate, the hedgerow is as great an inspiration as Constance Spry or Gertrude Jekyll, whose 1907 book, *Flower Decoration in the House,* continues to inspire. Seasonal flowers arranged in a natural way, in silver vases, Georgian wine glasses, painted Bristol glass carafes, tiny creamware mugs, or enormous Regency iron urns are still her preference. Nothing stiff or "floristy" is her motto. At home, her signature in summer is to arrange antique roses and belladonna lilies with aromatic leaves like mint, rosemary, verbena, fennel, and sage. In winter she forages for pyracantha berries, russet and ocher liquidambar leaves, rose hips, pine boughs, and shiny green holly.

Kate Reveals Her Flower Secrets:

Favorite flowers for picking: In Southern California, roses are blooming almost any time of the year. I'm fortunate. I love venturing into my garden year-round to pick flowers to bring into the house, the Cabana, and Bell Cottage.

The wide garden that flanks the main path toward the house includes mixed borders, each about twelve feet deep, and they are full of annuals, perennials, shrubs, and flowers I planted to pick for bouquets. The garden flourishes with roses and campanula, irises, feverfew, euphorbia, narcissus, and plectranthus. There are Renga, Oriental, and Crinum lilies. Mackaya bella, plumbago, clematis, and jasmine festoon borders, the fences, and walls. And there are masses of green and colored foliage, which are the structure in my arrangements.

Attractive leaves and blooms: Some of the best ornamental flowers for cutting come from our garden shrubs. Camellias, hydrangeas of several varieties, viburnum, and ligustrum provide very beautiful blooms and often some fragrance.

Fragrance, always: I have hedges of star jasmine along the length of my driveway, a beautifully scented backdrop to the border garden. The perfume of the tiny white flowers combines with that of my madonna lilies and the roses that wreathe the beds with all shades of pink and coral blossoms, and on warm sunny mornings, the aroma is as strong in the garden as it is when I combine them indoors. I have planted several types of lavender and scented geraniums along the edges of my paths, and when we brush against them, their foliage releases another layer of heavenly fragrance that combines with that of the blooming flowers. Plants that deliver their bouquet at night are a treasure in the garden, too. I love my bowering brugmansia, with its golden trumpets, the night-scented jasmine that makes up for its rather raggedy appearance with its powerful scent, and the old-fashioned stock (Matthiola incana) that will saturate its surroundings with a sweet odor of cloves. Scented flowers, especially those that climb, are good choices to plant outside a window that can sit open in your house. The wisteria and jasmine that

twine around my bedroom window transport me in the mornings with their fragrance. All of the places where we sit in the garden have citrus trees around them, and for a few months of the year, they are better than any expensive bottle of perfume. Cutting all of these things and bringing them indoors is a sweet pleasure, for they satisfy two of our senses, with their loveliness and their scent tying us again to the beauty of nature.

I let the flowers dictate the style: Some flowers, such as white or pale pink roses look wonderful in pretty and romantic bouquets that would suit a bride. I often add sprigs of fresh mint among the flowers. Camelias with their shiny leaves are elegant, and fragrant Philadelphus is charming, with pretty leaves and lovely white flowers.

Venturing into the vegetable garden: Another favorite area of the garden to mine for arrangements is my vegetable garden. I love the aromatic herbs like fennel or marjoram with pink roses in an antique silver vase. Broad outer cabbage leaves, replete with worm and snail holes, are dramatic, and I love ruby chard and pale grey artichoke leaves, sprays of rosemary, great bunches of mint, and trailing vines with purple beans still attached. They make unexpected combinations of fabulous foliage reminiscent of Dutch paintings of the seventeenth century. They deserve a large terra-cotta urn or a Wedgwood black basalt pitcher. I also have a great fondness for fragrant flowering stems of herbs like fennel or dill. Vegetables that have bolted, like carrots with their froth of white flowers, and chard with its drooping seedheads and the magnificent giant thistle flowers of artichokes, are as good sitting indoors in one of my tall flared–neck vases as they are in their raised beds in the garden.

Growing for cutting: My sheltered raised vegetable beds, protected with nets from birds, have also become a place where I grow flowers for cutting. The soil is the richest there, and seeds of some of my favorite campanula and feverfew have made their way via the birds to grow between the tomatoes and strawberries. I've not had the heart to take them out. They fill my vases very nicely so that my borders are not robbed of all the best blooms. I love delphiniums for their gorgeous blue tones and their tall elegant stems of blooms. I select flowers for cutting that have strong stems. I plant flowers like penstemon, Campanula americana, euphorbias, single fuchsias with their bells of purple and red, scabiosa, nigella, persicaria, and plumbago because they combine so beautifully in bouquets with my roses. Many of these are traditional English garden flowers, rarely available commercially.

Seasonal gifts: When most of the blossoms have faded in the borders and the vegetable garden has been cleared for the next season's plantings, I rely on fruits and berries and colored foliage to fill my vases inside. Enormous branches from my fig trees, laden with green or purple fruit, and their graphic emerald leaves will transform a room when arranged in a large cobalt-colored glass jug. The oranges, lemons, limes, mandarins, clementines, bergamots, and Buddha's hands are piled in bowls along with some of their glossy foliage where they can be enjoyed for their form, their scent and their taste. Persimmons and apples, quince and cherimoya fill my eighteenth-century Chinese export punchbowls when they are ripe, too. And in the autumn, my favorite time of year, the pyracantha berries, the rose hips, and the branches from the burgundy liquidambar and Chinese pistachio trees all find their way inside. They are ravishing along with the bursting seeds from the ligustrum and Iris foetidus, resplendent with the odd rose plucked because it was lonely in the garden. Oakleaf hydrangeas with their occasional crimson leaf and parchment dried flowers stand alone in tall vases in my sitting room, and boughs from our native oaks, with their green capped acorns, bring a kind of austere natural architecture indoors. The richness of the season reminds us, even here in Southern California, that there are natural cycles in our year.

Favorite native flowers: I love oak leaf hydrangeas in the fall as they turn red, burgundy, and gold. Acorns from native oaks with some of the golden leaves attached will bring the season inside, too.

Quiet winter: We are fortunate that our garden is vividly green all year. But in the winter, it's quiet and a single rose is a treasure to bring in the house. There are wonderful green branches, and some bulbs and hellebores, but in March things start to burst into flower.

We are organic. A rich layer of compost will nourish the soil from the top, keep the plants' roots cool, and help to prevent water evaporation.

I use only slow-release organic and completely natural fertilizers. Bat guano, fish emulsion, and worm castings are my favorites. The roses and camellias get a little extra help, but I don't like to push the blooms too much.

Leaves are lovely: Grow plenty of interesting foliage, two or three colors and textures all mixed are as interesting as roses. Holly is a beautiful glossy dark green and will last for weeks.

Daffodils and jonquils: I plant bulbs as well as perennials and annuals for cutting and to have plants that come into bloom through the season. I like classical trumpet daffodils for their bold yellow that announces spring and their noble stance in the garden bed. Jonquils find their way onto my dressing table, where they sit sweetly in one of my little painted glass vases. But the bluebells are my favorites. We grow Scilla hispanica, as the stronger scented English variety does not naturalize here. They have colonized my shade garden, filling in all of the interstitial spaces around the oaks and camellias, blooming around the bases of the Annabelles as their spring green leaves just begin to push out. Their sharp purplish blue shows up well at this point in the garden, and the thousands of blooms tide us over until the rest of the plants come to take their turn.

Sturdy garden tools: I have baskets full of sharpened secateurs and strong clippers, all carefully maintained and sharpened. One of my favorite professional-grade tools is a long, lightweight rose pruner with a blade that holds the flower after I cut it. This saves having to battle twigs and thorns to get those out-of-reach roses. I have two of these pruners; one is three feet long, the other six feet, which helps to reach vines and climbers, as well.

I wish you happy gardening.

STYLE SOURCES: A WORLD OF ANTIQUES, ART, AND TEXTILES

Kate's favorite international antique dealers, design stores, markets, art sources, country barns, antique textile experts, auction houses, style boutiques, and essential insider sources for beautiful objects, extraordinary furniture, and finds to treasure and enjoy.

Since she was a university student there, London has been Kate Stamps's favorite and most fruitful source for antiques. There are fewer shops in London now than there were then, but there are still wonderful concentrations along Pimlico Road and Lillie Road and Church Street N.W.8. Portobello Market thrives on Saturday mornings, although Bermondsey and Camden Lock continue now in a much reduced state. Kate suggests journeying into the countryside to find treasures in villages and market towns and extraordinary dealers in out of the way corners.

These are Kate's selections of the best dealers in London:

James Graham-Stewart

89-91 Scrubs Lane
www.jamesgrahamstewart.com
James has consistently the most interesting antiques anywhere. They vary from the grandest country house pieces with impeccable provenance to the perfect painted Regency chest of drawers. He has a discerning eye for everything, and you will find glorious carpets, paintings, and mirrors along with the furniture. Everything has character and soul.

The Lacquer Chest

75 Kensington Church Street
www.lacquerchest.com
The Lacquer Chest is a place to find the most charming accessory, a bit of creamware, an embroidered picture, a piece of treen, a small painted table. The shelves are always filled and the walls packed with thrilling things, a proper antique shop.

Reindeer Antiques

81 Kensington Church Street
www.reindeerantiques.co.uk
Peter, the owner, has beautiful, interesting, and fine furniture, and always a few surprises, like an agate-handled gilded silver dessert service in its original canteen. Most of his furniture is serious and brown, which Kate loves, but there are crumbling giltwood gothic rent tables and eighteenth-century painted commodes hiding there, too!

Humphrey Carrasco

702 Havelock Terrace, Battersea, by appointment
www.humphreycarrasco.com
Everything at Humphrey Carrasco is pure and perfect in its own right. Dark and massive early bookcases are balanced out with delicate and serpentine Regency library chairs. An ebony bull's-eye mirror silently watches your progress through the shop, a seventeenth-century oil painting on board depicts a country estate, made to show the great good fortune of the landowner. Most of the antiques here are quite austere, perfect in combination with modern things, as their shapes are clean and restrained.

Adam Calvert Bentley

www.hlbentley.co.uk, by appointment.
Adam is a young dealer with a wonderful eye for the quirky and decorative. His showroom is tucked away in Battersea, in a kind of rough and ready storage facility, but you forget that the minute he opens his metal front door and you enter a treasure trove. Small painted tables, parcel gilt commodes, gouache still-life paintings, you might find anything in his quickly changing and sumptuous collection.

McWhirter Morris and Alex di Caraci

11 Langton Street
www.mcwhirtermorris.com
James McWhirter and Sarah Morris are dealers and decorators, and they always have the most carefully chosen things that are designed to transform a room from something commonplace to something exceptional. Framed nineteenth-century Moroccan tile panels, pristine and delicate French rattan side tables, robust paintings of nineteenth-century actors, tiny wood carvings of Indian grandees. All on several floors in Chelsea.

Fisher London

65 Gray's Inn Road
www.fisher-london.com
You will always find interesting watercolors and small objects of interest at Hilary's shop, but she specializes in the glass and accessories to make a dinner table perfect. Bristol blue, cobalt, Irish, Georgian, Champagne and wine, hock and port,

all the glasses you could possibly need, plus the decanters and jugs and pitchers to go with them. It is the best spot to find a present for a wedding or a friend, and best of all, a present for yourself. What a pleasure it is to use these things every day.

Nicholas Gifford-Mead

www.nicholasgiffordmead.co.uk
Nicholas specializes in the most beautiful chimney pieces. He has many unusual examples, mostly English, Italian, and French from all periods and of all materials. But he also has fireplace tools, garden furniture and ornaments, and lovely sculpture. The quality here is impeccable.

Kate Thurlow

Gallery Forty One
www.katethurlow.co.uk
Kate deals by appointment now, and she specializes in interesting and early antiques. Everything she has seems to possess a sculptural quality and adds spirit and soul to a room.

King's Road:

Julia Boston

588 King's Road
www.juliaboston.com
Julia has been in her corner on the King's Road for quite a long time, and she is famous for her tapestries and tapestry cartoons, but she also has elegant and refined English and Continental furniture and beautiful accessories.

Guinevere Antiques

574-580 King's Road
www.guinevere.co.uk
Guinevere has been on the King's Road for ages, too, and really is a glamorous department store for antiques and decorative objects. You will find interesting pieces of furniture, paintings, tableware, carpets, and their own beautifully hand-dyed linens, as well as exotic and unusual things from every period.

On the Pimlico Road and Ebury Street and Bourne Street, there are wonderful shops like:

Hilary Batstone

84 Bourne Street
www.hilarybatstone.com
Hilary has been in this business for quite a long time, and her shop has evolved in a lovely way.

French and Italian things are mixed with the English and Scandinavian. There are treasures from the '30s–but it might be the 1730s, 1830s, or 1930s. There is always the glitter of silver in a fine plate of mirror, a pair of Baguès sconces or a Directoire plateau, and glamour in platinum satin upholstery. And Hilary is the mother of Rose Uniacke, whose chic gallery/antique shop is just around the corner at 76 Pimlico Road.

Timothy Langston Fine Art and Antiques

198 Ebury Street
www.timothylangston.com
Tim specializes in the kind of antiques and decorative objects one wishes to see in every London drawing room. Black lacquer Chinoiserie side tables, peacock blue porcelain lamps, Georgian portraits of grand ladies in their pearls and taffetas. And there are plenty of French and Italian things, too, and beautiful mirrors and botanical paintings in églomisé frames. All refined and interesting.

Robert Kime

190-192 Ebury Street
www.robertkime.com
World famous for his decorating and fabrics, Robert is also a wonderful antiques dealer. From Vietnamese funerary urns to Venetian embroidered panels and even Egyptian rarities, there is only gorgeousness here.

Tarquin Bilgen

227 Ebury Street
www.tarquinbilgen.com
Tiny and select, Tarquin will always have something to take your breath away. Rare things and objects of extraordinary beauty, absolutely everything is worth a second or third look. And then you can take it home!

Howe London

93 Pimlico Road
www.howelondon.com
Christopher has an interesting eye and assembles and combines pure eighteenth-century antiques with Scandinavian carpets from the 1950s, pristine Albini wicker lobster pot ottomans from the '50s, bentwood tables by Thonet, and the list goes on! Every object has a point of view, and Christopher has his own line of upholstered furniture. His tufted dining chairs are my favorites, made by hand in a beautiful manner and comfortable enough for dinner parties that go on for hours.

Jamb

95-97 Pimlico Road
www.jamb.co.uk
Charlotte and Will have a very special place in the world of decoration in London. Their knowledge and ability to come up with the most desirable things set them apart. They are two separate shops, one dealing in antiques and the other in their special reproductions. They have a vast collection of distinguished chimney pieces and if you can't find one in their stock to suit your measurements, they will make one for you.

Anthony Outred

74 Pimlico Road
www.outred.co.uk
The rare things to be found at Anthony Outred are exquisitely beautiful. Lacca povera cabinets, colonial carved tables, botanical models, ivory inlaid vargueno, anything rare and desirable is likely to be discovered here, but in addition, they stock fabulous brass door hardware. Beehive knobs, gently worn Georgian doorknobs the color of rose gold, Victorian gothic towel bars. These quiet but elegant hardware fittings change a room in important but subtle ways.

Sibyl Colefax and John Fowler

89-91 Pimlico Road
www.sibylcolefax.com
Of course, these two names are the most famous in the pantheon of English decoration, along with that of the unnamed partner, Nancy Lancaster. This business is separate from the fabric company (although they will reproduce some of the great classics now discontinued by the fabric house) and relocated here from the old Brook Street. They reference all of the great work of the past in the stock they carry, but they also look forward with lovely paintings, contemporary pieces, and surprising departures from what we think of as English Country House style.

Christopher Butterworth

71 Pimlico Road
www.christopherbutterworth.net
One may hesitate to recommend Christopher, because his tiny shop, run by the redoubtable Nella, to whom we are all grateful, is a veritable Aladdin's cave. But it is well worth the effort, because every single thing in those stacks and piles is a treasure. This is an essential stop in the world for lighting, whether it is an immense Colza lamp or a supercool bit of '60s painted pottery to a refined giltwood sconce from Italy. Wonderful.

Other shops in London:

Lillie Road: Lillie Road is not the obvious upmarket antiques street in London, but many designers visit here. Things fly out the doors on this street to the more glamorous showrooms a few miles away and into beautiful rooms by the world's best designers. Not to be missed.

Andrew Bewick Antiques

287 Lillie Road
I love Andrew and Jonathan's point of view. I have found French Algerian cabinets, Regency painted chests of drawers, seventeenth-century Persian mirrors, Maltese inlaid tables, and so many other treasures here.

Shane Meredith

295 Lillie Road
Everything from crystal ship chandeliers to Venetian lanterns to Directoire bookcases, always surprising.

Dorian Caffot de Fawes

313 Lillie Road
www.dorian-antiques.com
Glamour and refinement. Mostly continental and twentieth century.

M. Charpentier Antiques

284 Lillie Road
www.mcharpentier.com
Lots of the best French antiques, from two sisters brilliantly following in the footsteps of their legendary mother.

Maison Artefact

273 Lillie Road
www.maisonartefact.com
Quiet and serene and thoughtful. Graceful French and Scandinavian painted things punctuated with the occasional surprise. I always find something here.

Woodnutt Antiques

271 Lillie Road
www.woodnutantiques.com
Horn cups, silver cocktail shakers, glamorous ice buckets, cranberry glass match holders with silver strikes, a favorite lamp in the form of a carved lotus, small things that evoke another age, another time. Presents you always mean to give

away, but you end up wrapping for yourself. And Piers is the nicest man around.

Cubbit Antiques
289 Lillie Road
www.cubbitantiques.com
Hurry, hurry, it won't last more than a minute here! Architectural and garden things and plenty more.

Puckhaber Decorative Antiques
281 Lillie Road
www.puckhaberdecorativeantiques.com
Wonderful and constantly changing. Not their usual thing, but I bought my favorite upholstered chair here. You will find lovely pieces.

269 Antiques
269 Lillie Road
Mark has chandeliers and mirrors, furniture and bibelot, but I can't resist the upholstered furniture. Don't wait to think, just buy it. It won't be there tomorrow.

Matthew Upham Antiques
312 Lillie Road
www.matthewupham.com
Chandeliers, chandeliers, chandeliers. Thrilling.

Nimmo & Spooner
277 Lillie Road
www.nimmoandspooner.co.uk
Interesting varieties of unexpected charm. A lovely point of view.

In the English Countryside:

Dean Antiques
Herefordshire
www.deanantiques.co.uk
Comprehensive, imaginative, and amazing. Really only furniture, but his selection is diverse. If a client wants an interesting, glamorous, and comfortable sofa, Dean will have one. Howard upholstery, gothic tables, Regency library chairs, gothic metal doors rescued from an abandoned garden. Everything you might need. Or want.

Blank Canvas Antiques/Andy Gibbs
23-24 Brookend Street, Ross-on-Wye, Herefordshire

I have a very soft spot for Andy. He is a lovely man, with two of the most charming little boys you can imagine, and he has built one of the best antiques businesses in just a few years with honest dedication. I couldn't possibly list everything he can find, but I have bought the loveliest chairs, carpets, bookcases, sofas, tables, and beds from him. Look carefully and be happy to spend the day.

Max Rollitt
Yavington Barn,
Lovington Lane, Avington, Hampshire
Decorator/dealers have a special place in this business, but Max Rollitt is one of a very few who get it completely right. Rich color, clever and amusing collections, charm, and thoughtfulness abound. Max can supply practical solutions for all of your decorating problems, but combined with a touch of whimsy with solid knowledge.

Edward Hurst
Manor Farm
Telegraph Street, Shroton,
Near Blandford Forum, Dorset
www.edwardhurst.com
In some ways, the most inspirational of all the dealers today. How do you combine asceticism with a kind of earthiness? It is an art and Edward Hurst's effortless aesthetic is reinforced by tremendous experience and erudition.

David Bedale
Grove House
Mobberley, Cheshire
www.davidbedale.com
David's selections are magic. If there is a linen press, it is pollarded oak with a tiny gothic detail below the cornice. A William IV armchair has gilded legs and once belonged to the Royal Family. The upholstered chair is stamped Howard, circa 1880. The loveliest quality, beautifully chosen.

Country towns known for their antique shops:

Petworth, West Sussex
Tetbury, Gloucestershire
Stow-on-the-Wold, Gloucestershire

charming bookshop. Brown Water Books has literary fiction with a southern accent, both classic and new, the kind of books everyone should be reading.

Kinsey Marable
www.privatelibraries.com
If I ever needed to replace the contents of my own library, this is where I could do it. You could build an entire collection of the esoteric and amusing books on culture and design found here.

Textile Dealers:

Peta Smyth
42 Moreton Street Pimlico SW1V 2PB
www.petasmyth.com
The very, very best. Erudition, soul, and beauty in a serene and inviting environment.

Katharine Pole
www.katharinepole.com
Here, there is tremendous variety and everything from bits for cushions to toile hangings for a complete bed.

Rhona Valentine
www.rhonavalentine.co.uk
Needlework, cushions, curtains, and wall hangings. The loveliest things.

Şeref Özen
sorugsandtextiles@gmail.com
The go-to place for suzanis; Middle Eastern, Caucasian, and Ottoman textiles; carpets, and pillows, exactly as described, and Seref supplies the best decorators.

Textile Trunk
www.textiletrunk.com
Really more like Mary Poppins' carpet bag, you can find everything online here. Useful treasures.

Carpets

Y&B Bolour
321 South Robertson Boulevard
Los Angeles
www.ybbolour.com
Mr. Bolour is the eminence grise of antique carpet dealers. I have been buying glorious Isfahans, Oushaks, Ziegler, Aubusson, Bessarabian, and European carpets from his gallery for many years. He also has the most gorgeous tapestries, wall hangings, and cushions, all beautiful and rare.

Joshua Lumley
Stonebridge Barn Egerton, Kent
www.joshualumley.com
Joshua has lovely carpets, both decorative and fine, including European and hard-to-find midcentury flat weaves. After leaving Sotheby's as Head of Department in European rugs, he has established himself in Kent, where he has a lovely showroom.

US DEALERS:

Tom Stansbury Antiques
466 Old Newport Blvd., Newport Beach, California
www.tomstansburyantiques.com.
In the business for more than forty years, Tom's contacts and sources are second to none. Old Hollywood estates (try Sister Parish, Sophia Loren, Debbie Reynolds, among others) all end up in Tom's shops. Stacked one upon the other, you will find export china, Derby, creamware, Vieux Paris porcelain. There are embroidery and needlework pictures and eighteenth century furniture from all over the world. Leather bound books, Venetian consoles, and paintings you could only dream of.

Pat McGann
746 North La Cienega Blvd. Los Angeles
www.patmcganngallery.com
Pat has interesting and varied stock. Intriguing oil paintings and beautiful textiles, and stacks of pillows. Things from around the globe and around the corner. A wonderful eye, and with great staying power on La Cienega!

Blackman Cruz
836 North Highland Avenue Los Angeles
www.blackmancruz.com
Adam and David have been leading the design crowd for many years. Their gallery, arranged on several floors, is replete with staggeringly good things. Everything has a distinct point of view, but nothing is too precious. Just the mix one wants to live with.

Wendy Foster
516 San Ysidro Road, Montecito, California
www.wendyfoster.com
In addition to fabulous women's clothing, Wendy Foster has a second floor filled with unique objects for the house and garden. There are bedlinens, moroccan carpets, decoupage trays, and a great selection of tableware. When you can't carry anything else,

go down to the café to enjoy a glass of wine with your lunch. An institution.

Ann Koerner Antiques
New Orleans
www.annkoerner.com
Ann has always had the most wonderful artist's eye for beauty and rarity. She stands out from the crowd in New Orleans.

Balzac Antiques
New Orleans
www.balzacantiques.com
Such lovely things, both charming and fine, with that interesting and unique New Orleans accent. Sarah has always had things to dream of.

KRB Designs
138 East 74th Street, New York, New York
www.krbnyc.com
Vivacious Kate Brodsky, (Odom and Kate's niece and designer Suzanne Rheinstein's daughter) has created a shop of glamour and flair. Her first boutique was a small jewel box, and now, in her new 74th Street location, Kate's larger shop is a treasure trove. Marian McEvoy's collages in cork and pressed leaves and flowers are favorites, along with her painted lampshades. Frances Palmer's vases, Saved's yak and cashmere throws, and custom linens from Leontine are essential luxuries. Kate also has a well curated selection of antiques.

Bardith
135 1/2 East 79th Street, New York, New York
www.bardith.com
Bardith, which has been in business since 1964, is the very best place in the States to find extraordinary porcelain and pottery. They have Regency Derby vases that might have come from the grandest country house or a set of Wedgwood creamware plates which will dress a supper table perfectly. Bardith will make a collector of anyone who walks through the door.

My favorite fabrics in the world seem to be designed by women, and I go to them over and over for chintzes and documents, embossed velvets and serious stripes:

Tissus d'Hélenè
421 Design Center East
Chelsea Harbour, London SW10 0XF
sales@tissusdhelene.co.uk

Sabina Fay Braxton
38 Avenue Jean Jaurès
94110
Arcueil, France
www.sabinafaybraxton.com

Lisa Fine
www.lisafinetextiles.com

Nicole Fabre
www.nicolefabredesigns.com

Namay Samay
www.namaysamay.com

Idarica Gazzoni
Arjumand's World
www.arjumandsworld.com

Watts of Westminster
www.watts1874.co.uk

Chelsea Textiles
www.chelseatextiles.com

Jean Monro
www.jeanmonro.com

Nathalie Farman-Farma
Décors Barbares
www.decorsbarbares.com

And there are a few favorite gentlemen, too:

Robert Kime
www.robertkime.com

Christopher Moore
www.thetoileman.com

Hazelton House
www.hazeltonhouse.com

ACKNOWLEDGMENTS

To Laurel Myers Tagaras, without whom absolutely nothing would happen, and to her husband, Yiorgos, who kindly tolerates all of the mad designers.

To Wendy Myers, Jane Fehrenbacher, Julie Simms, Peggy Christ, and Hao Hoang, who form the core of Stamps & Stamps, and to all of the other staff who have contributed so much over the years to what we do.

To Jean Randazzo, who is a tried and true friend, client, and inspiration as a photographer.

To Marina Khrustaleva, thank you for always pointing out the perfect light and for your fabulous photography assistance, and Vladimir Paperny for the essential tutorials in photo editing.

To Ben Pope and Carrie Worthen, who in addition to being great friends, gentle critics, and wise advisers, were the source of all camera essentials for a neophyte photographer.

To Pilar Viladas, who has been a dear friend, an advocate for our work, a favorite guest, and a clear pair of rational eyes. It always feels like home when you are around.

To Diane Dorrans Saeks, who suggested the entire project, and whose confident guidance and powerful aesthetic made the book what it is.

To Paul McKevitt, who constantly amazed me with the art direction that sets our book apart and makes it so interesting and appealing.

To Ellen Nidy, you made pulling all of the threads together seem easy, when we know it was hard. Our induction into your world was great fun and a painless education.

To Charles Miers, who had the patience to look at the entire preliminary mock-up and still say yes.

To Tim Street-Porter and Annie Kelly, friends and inspiring guides from the beginning.

To Annie Higgins, for many things, but in addition, for the brainstorming that led to the title.

To my dearest friends Janine Ulfane and Hugh Henry, my anchors in England.

To our families, and especially to Suzanne Rheinstein, who gave us our start in Los Angeles.

To Mr. Big, who sat every day with me through the endless photo editing, I miss you terribly.

CREDITS/COPYRIGHT

First published in the United States of America in 2021 by
Rizzoli International Publications, Inc.
300 Park Avenue South
New York, NY 10010
www.rizzoliusa.com

Publisher: Charles Miers
Editor: Ellen Nidy
Design: Paul McKevitt, subtitleny.com
Production Manager: Barbara Sadick
Managing Editor: Lynn Scrabis

Printed in China

2020 2021 2022 2023 2024 / 10 9 8 7 6 5 4 3 2 1

ISBN: 978-0-8478-6864-3
Library of Congress Control Number: 2020950516

Visit us online:
Facebook.com / RizzoliNewYork
instagram.com/rizzolibooks
twitter.com/Rizzoli_Books
pinterest.com/rizzolibooks
youtube.com/user/RizzoliNY
issuu.com/rizzoli